720.92 SAN

JOEL SANDERS

582866

ONE WEEK LOAN

D1586758

WITHDRAWN FROM LIBRARY STOCK

009604450

JOEL SANDERS WRITINGS AND PROJECTS

FOREWORD BY TERENCE RILEY
INTRODUCTION BY JOSEPH ROSA

THE MONACELLI PRESS

First published in the United States of America in 2004 by
The Monacelli Press, Inc.
902 Broadway, New York, New York 10010.

Copyright © 2004 The Monacelli Press, Inc.
Text copyright © 2004 Joel Sanders

All rights reserved under International and Pan-American
Copyright Conventions. No part of this book may be reproduced or
utilized in any form or by any means, electronic or mechanical,
including photocopying, recording, or by any information storage
and retrieval system, without permission in writing from the publisher.
Inquiries should be sent to The Monacelli Press, Inc.

Library of Congress Cataloging-in-Publication Data
Sanders, Joel, date.
Joel Sanders : writings and projects / Joel Sanders ; foreword by
Terence Riley ; introduction by Joseph Rosa.
p. cm.
Includes bibliographical references.
ISBN 1-58093-143-X
1. Sanders, Joel, date– —Catalogs. 2. Architecture—United
States—20th century—Catalogs. 3. Architecture—United
States—21st century—Catalogs. I. Title.
NA737.S318A4 2004
720'.92—dc22   2004013667

Printed and bound in Italy

Designed by Claudia Brandenburg, Language Arts

WRITINGS   PROJECTS

ACKNOWLEDGMENTS

Hindsight affords the luxury of taking stock of the past but risks retroactively imposing a coherent narrative on a messy reality. While a series of recurring themes and issues has contributed to the trajectory of my practice, chance circumstances—from the vagaries of the global economy to casual conversations at cocktail parties— have factored equally in bringing to fruition the projects in these pages. Architecture is not a linear process, nor is it produced by a single author: more often than not it is a haphazard enterprise that reflects the input of multiple protagonists, from clients to contractors, colleagues to office staff.

I must credit the international roster of hardworking architects and interns who have patiently worked with me, toiling long hours over the drawings and models reproduced in this book. Although the talented young associates are too many to list, I am especially grateful for the close collaboration offered by Marc Tsurumaki, Christoph Roselius, and Brian Kimura.

The built work would not be possible without supportive clients like Marilyn Ziment, John Vitale, Andrew and Li-Ying Lee, Charles and Jane Worthington, and Stelios Haji-Ioannou, all of whom trusted my studio to execute less than conventional design ideas. I have been lucky enough to team up with two dedicated contractors, Saif Sumaida and Charles Choi, both craftsmen who value design integrity over the bottom line.

Every project shown here originated as a built commission, but many remained unrealized. Supportive curators like Mark Robbins, Donald Albrecht, Memos Phillipidis, Terry Riley, and Joe Rosa have invited me to exhibit these projects, bringing them back to life and providing me and my staff with the incentive to redraw and, in some cases, elaborate the designs. Terry Riley, Joe Rosa, and Mark Robbins were also kind enough to contribute to this volume.

Over the years, I have reaped many benefits from teaching in stimulating academic environments. Special thanks to my many colleagues at Princeton University, Parsons School of Design, and Yale University, including Robert Gutman, Alan Colquhoun, Karen Van Lengen, Peter Wheelwright, Silvia Kolbowski, Natalie Fizer, Robert Stern, Steven Harris, Louise Harpman, Deborah Berke, and Peggy Deamer. Close friends Russell Ferguson, Karen Higa, John Keenan, David Joselitz, James Shaheen, and John Lindell have offered both emotional and intellectual sustenance over the years. Louise Kramer, Steven Bloomfield, and Paul Gunther gave love and support in even the most trying moments. I am especially indebted to Diana Fuss. Though we come from different disciplines, our mutual interest in the way space shapes human experience has allowed us to conduct an ongoing and intellectually stimulating dialogue.

I developed the concept for this book during a residency at the MacDowell Colony. Generous grants from the Larry Kramer Foundation and the Arcus Foundation supported its publication. Many thanks to Andrea Monfried, my editor at The Monacelli Press, and the talented book designer Claudia Brandenburg. Both have patiently guided me through the complicated and often challenging process of assembling this volume. In my office, Edowa Shimizu took on the daunting task of coordinating the visual materials.

This book is dedicated to the memory of my friend John Pozzi and my grandmother Sonia Sadofsky, two departed souls who both showed me that surfaces are never only skin deep.

FOREWORD TERENCE RILEY
THE PHILIP JOHNSON CHIEF CURATOR, DEPARTMENT OF ARCHITECTURE AND DESIGN
THE MUSEUM OF MODERN ART, NEW YORK

In this volume, Joel Sanders represents and refines his projects and arguments of the last decade. Sanders's architectural and written work is worthy of close study for a number of reasons, which I would summarize as his *reflexive criticality*. In terms of criticality, it is not possible to engage the issues at hand—the politics and aesthetics of gender, family and society, public and private—without a familiarity with the philosophical and political literature that has defined the debates of the 1990s and early 2000s. Sanders's work generously speaks to the writers and thinkers who have influenced his own point of view and makes room for other voices as well, and it does so without the rancor that has characterized the debate of these same issues in other media.

The reflexivity, however, comes not in the acknowledgment but in the response. Sanders is first and foremost an architect; his skill is his ability to transform ideas into material and space. Architecture is a means of expression far more abstract than language, combining as it does both the visual and the literary. Sanders's work delights in this kind of eye-mind interaction but speaks to the purely architectonic as well, the self-referential parlance of architecture. As Ludwig Wittgenstein observed, after his sole foray into architecture, it is much more difficult to be an architect than a philosopher.

It is this back and forth between ideas about architecture and architecture about ideas that makes Sanders's work so important. Neither subsumes the other; both are utterly dependent on the other. While no idea can fully describe or supplant the many joys of architecture, architecture without ideas is not worthy of the name.

PREFACE JOEL SANDERS

Since the early 1990s, my work—speculative and built—has attempted to register the complex intersection between architecture and society, taking into account the cultural shifts that shape and in turn are shaped by the built environment. The chronological organization of the work included in this volume, both writings and projects, attempts to highlight the connections that link culture and space via the evolution of a series of recurrent themes and problems: visuality and the senses, gender and human identity, disciplinary rifts between architects and interior decorators, and the reciprocal relationship between technology and the body.

SIGHT SPECIFIC

Although we generally think of buildings as objects to be looked at, built structures are also instruments that help to regulate *how* we look—at objects, people, and landscapes. My early residential projects explore this question of visuality and architecture, looking at the ways in which dwellings, by framing visual relationships, help to define social interactions. Projects like the Kyle residence in Houston (1993) and Sight Specific (1994), commissioned for an exhibition at the Wexner Center, challenge the traditional conception of the American home as a self-sufficient, free-standing entity insulated from the outside world. Instead they acknowledge how windows—from double-hung panes to television and computer monitors—permit the relay of the gaze (voyeuristic and surveilling) and simultaneously allow a host of actual and electronic images to penetrate the sanctity of the home. These designs reconfigure elements borrowed from both high modernist and conventional house plans in order to promote more open scopic, spatial, and ultimately, social relationships among owners, neighbors, and the world.

The views of nature framed by the apertures of dwellings are themselves "human-made": despite their naturalistic pretensions, residential landscapes, like homes, are carefully designed constructions. The Kyle residence

and Sight Specific introduce a feature that reappears in Peekskill Artists' Live-Work Housing (1994–96), the House for a Bachelor (1997–99), and elsewhere—the lawn as an objectified artificial surface that, from the perspective of the domestic interior, behaves as a framing device that edits unsightly views of the surrounding suburban environment. In these residential projects, vision, nature, and dwelling are dynamic and interdependent fabrications.

BACHELORS OF ARCHITECTURE

An examination of the question of visuality and architecture leads, inevitably, to the politics of vision, a topic that underscores the intersection between space, vision, and gender. In 1996, I started to focus on these issues in *Stud: Architectures of Masculinity,* a collection of essays and projects by architects, artists, and cultural theorists. My introduction to the book, included in this volume, discussed the ordinary but overlooked spaces in our daily lives—homes, bathrooms, parks, gyms—that help to engineer male identity. Indebted to gender theory's notion of identity as "performance," my text outlined various strategies—from organizing the gaze to demarcating boundaries—that allow built structures to set the stage for the enactment of manhood.

Stud broadened the scope of architecture from the permanent walls erected by architects to include the ephemeral fabrics, furniture, and accessories traditionally associated with interior decorators. My essay "Berggasse 19: Inside Freud's Office," cowritten with Diana Fuss, brings together these themes—identity, interior design, power, and gender—in a close reading of Freud's office. The spatial organization of this suite of rooms, densely populated with his collection of Egyptian and Roman antiquities, prescribed and made possible the psychoanalytic relationship between doctor and patient.

Freud's home/office was not the only male domestic interior documented in *Stud*. Focusing on what some would consider a contradiction in terms—male domesticity—the first chapter was devoted to bachelor pads, exclusively male domains popularized in the postwar media and press. Soon after completing *Stud,* my theoretical interests converged with my practice: I received two residential commissions, one urban and one suburban, for single male clients. Both the Lee loft in New York (1997–99) and the House for a Bachelor in Minneapolis explore the reciprocity between cladding and clothing—a theme that has become an ongoing preoccupation in my design work. Whether hard or soft, interior or exterior, the materials that clad people and buildings are coded surfaces that enable the articulation of human identity.

CURTAIN WARS

Two years after the topic of interiors first appeared on my radar screen during the process of editing *Stud,* I began to focus on the underdog status of interior design. Why, I wondered, did my architectural training leave me unprepared to execute the increasing number of interiors commissions that entered my practice, jobs that required me not only to move walls and plumbing but to pick fabrics and furnishings? "Curtain Wars: Architects, Decorators, and the Twentieth-Century Domestic Interior," the title of a conference I organized at Parsons School of Design in 1996 and of an essay reprinted here, attempted to account for the conflicts between architects and decorators, the "wars" that are waged over something as seemingly innocuous as a curtain.

Although architects and decorators perform overlapping and often identical functions, they have, since the emergence of the professional decorator in the early twentieth century, occupied antagonistic camps. Popularly held conceptions about the nature of architecture and gender continue to bolster this rift. Architects, engaged in an ostensibly intellectual and masculine pursuit, organize space by manipulating permanent elements and materials (structure and walls); decorators, involved in a task associated with feminine artifice and masquerade, adorn rooms with ephemeral elements (soft fabrics and movable furniture). In short, many of the superficial assumptions about both fields are themselves sustained by broad cultural stereotypes and anxieties about the nature of class, gender, and popular culture.

As the term "curtain wall" implies, architecture and decoration are not oppositional but interdependent. Another essay included in this book, "Ergotectonics," attempts to bridge this gap, outlining a design approach that blends the hard, space-defining surfaces favored by architects with the comfortable, humanly scaled elements typically employed by interior designers. Ergotectonics advocates the creation of flexible multipurpose environments responsive to the fluid nature of contemporary lifestyles.

Designed according to Ergotectonic principles, some of my subsequent projects—the Five Minute Bathroom (commissioned for *Wallpaper* magazine in 1999) and the Foundry in New York (2000–2001)—feature continuous folding surfaces, precisely molded to the contours of the body, that sensuously merge furniture and enclosure. Others, like the Vitale loft (1999–2000) and the Sands loft (2000), both in New York, propose living environments comprised of interconnected networks of surfaces, materials, and infrastructures (soft, wet, work, digital) that promote a variety of activities, rather than single-function rooms. All of these projects feature flexible screens and partitions that allow occupants to regulate publicity and privacy.

While early projects like the Lee loft and the House for a Bachelor were concerned with articulating maleness, these subsequent designs are increasingly concerned with permitting multiple identities. Changing demographics unite with new technologies to forge fluid domestic identities, transforming homes into multi-identity, multi-task environments. Recent projects respond to this trend by proposing truly flexible living landscapes that, over the course of a single day, allow men and women to take on a variety of roles, both domestic and professional, as partners, parents, and wage earners.

TACTILE TECHNOLOGIES

The most recent projects included in this volume apply Ergotectonic principles to nonresidential programs like salons, hotels, and schools; they also come full circle, returning to the questions of vision, voyeurism, and technology that informed my early thinking. However, in these later projects, my focus has expanded from an emphasis on vision to a consideration of the body's other senses, including touch and smell.

In considering buildings as objects to be seen, architects and occupants tend to forget that structures in general, and dwellings in particular, by their very nature shelter the most basic biological needs: eating, sleeping, washing, urinating, defecating, having sex. Architecture upholds a Western, ocular-centric tradition that privileges vision—affiliated with immaterial intellect—while bracketing out the other "higher" sense, hearing, along with the unruly "lower" senses—touch, taste, and smell, all associated with corruptible flesh. For example, two domestic spaces specifically dedicated to the satisfaction of bodily functions—kitchens and bathrooms—register our culture's deepest and most profound anxieties about the corporeal body. Bathrooms conjure the specter of sexuality and pleasure at the same time they signal the material presence of the corporeal body that produces waste. In a society saturated with unattainable images of physical perfection achieved through self-discipline and self-denial, kitchens also subliminally remind us of our carnal appetites. In fact, pioneering modernists like Adolf Loos and Le Corbusier embraced what was at the time considered a cutting-edge technology, plumbing, as an instrument for triumphing over abjection. They attempted to eradicate all traces of the corporeal body; not only could running water wash away human waste, but by cladding kitchens and bathrooms in impervious, often white surfaces, designers could foster the largely visual impression of cleanliness and hygiene.

My projects, on the other hand—the Vitale loft, the Five Minute Bathroom, and the Millennium residence (New York, 2001–2) among them—treat kitchens, bathrooms, and even closets as pivotal domestic zones that communicate with each other and with the rest of the home. Recognizing that Americans already lavish significant design dollars on these spaces, traditionally cordoned off from public view, these projects celebrate rather than disguise their associations with the body.

Some of my later designs attempt to take the exploration of the senses one step further by building on a theme—the reciprocal relationship between optical and tactile, virtual and actual space—that first became apparent as I prepared an essay about gyms. "A Site for Sore Eyes" argues that gyms and health clubs are singular programmatic types in which animated bodies come into direct contact with all the surfaces of architecture (walls, floors, and ceilings) as they encounter a host of virtual images, transmitted via mirrors, televisions, and even monitors embedded in exercise machines. Yet gyms are not the only places where vision and kinesthetics meet. Surfing the Internet while eating lunch at the office, talking on a cell phone while walking in the street, watching videos while having sex at home are only a few examples of how our sensory experiences are increasingly shaped by synesthetic experiences intensified by the proliferation of electronic images in each and every space of our lives. My most recent projects—the Access House in Georgia (2001–2), 24/7 Business Hotel for the Cooper-Hewitt Museum (2002–3), Fashion Institute of Technology competition in New York (2003), and Olympic Equestrian Facility on Staten Island (2003–)—take advantage of the ways in which technology facilitates such opportunities for full-bodied sensory experiences. These soft but wired environments in which the senses meet highlight the merging of architecture and technology, yet they are still informed by issues of vision and visuality, identity, and the interdependence of architecture and decoration—ongoing preoccupations now explored at a larger and more public scale.

FROM MODERNISM TO ERGOTECTONICS: THE WORK OF JOEL SANDERS JOSEPH ROSA

HELEN HILTON RAISER CURATOR OF ARCHITECTURE AND DESIGN

SAN FRANCISCO MUSEUM OF MODERN ART, SAN FRANCISCO

Through the filter of pedagogy and practice, architect Joel Sanders questions normative cultural assumptions concerning gender, identity, and visuality as they are transmitted through the conventions of architecture. Sanders reveals, inverts, and transposes such conventions in order to create new spatial and social relationships. Over the years, Sanders's writings and designs have evolved from a critique of the modernist tradition: his early works often reconfigured modernist precedents while his more recent projects invent a new aesthetic vocabulary and method for architectural production.

The architect's early interest in reevaluating modernism is exemplified in his design for the Kyle residence in Houston (1993), where he conceptually collages two of Mies van der Rohe's domestic prototypes, the freestanding house and the courtyard house, exemplified by the Farnsworth house (1950) and the Court House studies (c. 1930). In plan, the perimeter wall of the Court House demarcates the boundaries of the Kyle house; the Farnsworth house is transposed onto the streetfront. But in section, the deployment of the Mies houses is shifted: the Court House is partially recessed into the ground and the Farnsworth house sits above grade. Mies's influence is also evident in the way programs are dispersed. An internal monolithic service core containing the kitchen, bathroom, and fireplace—disposed as they are in the Farnsworth house—is canted and extruded from the rectangular form to create a visual barrier between house and street. Unlike the expansive natural setting of the Mies design, the rear garden of the Kyle residence is a synthetic landscape that gently rises to block the view of adjacent houses.

The idea of a synthetic landscape is developed in Sanders's House for a Bachelor on the outskirts of Minneapolis (1997–99), this time deployed as a commentary on how gender identity, like nature, is a fabrication. Sanders was commissioned to renovate a one-story ranch house typical of those in the suburban community, and at first glance the structure appears unchanged. However, on closer examination, it is clear that the house's existing facades function as cladding or "dressing" on what is essentially a modern house, masking—from the street—Sanders's drastic reconfiguration of the interior and rear garden.

Sanders revisits the suburban "finished basement" to produce a bachelor's master suite, which opens onto a recessed, two-story backyard. To provide privacy from adjacent neighbors, the back wall of the depressed garden, covered in Astroturf, rises at a steep angle to create an environment that, in effect, cocoons in suburbia the bachelor's existence. By excavating this backyard and rethinking the lower level of the house, Sanders's design results in a two-story modern home clad in the facades of a one-story ranch house. The concealment of the house's unorthodox interior spaces is a metanarrative for the client—a single gay man who resides in a mostly heterosexual subdivision. In this way, the House for a Bachelor capitalizes on and overturns the reputation of single men and women as destabilizing elements within the idealized setting of domestic suburban bliss.

While the House for a Bachelor can be viewed as a modern home in contextual drag, it also reveals Sanders's ability to generate a contemporary architectural vocabulary of self-contained forms able to coexist with and within other typologies or preexisting conditions, a theme he elaborates in two subsequent projects, the Vitale (1999–2000) and Sands (2000) lofts, both in New York. In high-rise buildings, the location of plumbing stacks often results in back-to-back kitchens and bathrooms. But in the Vitale loft, Sanders questions the convention of barriers that visually separate the bathroom from the kitchen by creating one contiguous platform that commands the space. The only opaque vertical barrier is a glass partition separating the kitchen counter from the shower/bath area of the platform. A single concrete surface bends and folds both "functions" together, blurring the social boundaries between these public and private spaces.

The insertion of such sculptural forms—merging furniture and enclosure, the scale of the body with the scale of a building—is further developed in later projects by Sanders, illustrating what he has come to define as Ergotectonics:

Devising domestic environments that promote fluid domestic identities depends on inventing a new design vocabulary that merges the best aspects of the divided worlds of architecture and decoration . . . Interior decoration and architecture will finally be understood as continuous practices.

Sanders's interest in Ergotectonics marks a shift in his methodology, away from the politics of constructing identity through gendered space and toward a consideration of the relationship between an androgynous body and its movement in space. This shift is often manifested in the design of monolithic pontoonlike forms that can be deployed in existing open spaces. In the Sands loft, Sanders creates a "leisure landscape," which spans the length of the loft; comprising kitchen, living/entertainment, bath, and master bedroom, it allows its owner to circulate between domestic programs unencumbered by dividing walls.

Sanders employs the leisure landscape concept—juxtaposing autonomous objects against existing environments—in a non-residential context at the Foundry (2000–2001), two adjacent residential buildings in New York. Sanders's white terrazzo surfaces, calibrated to the contours of moving and seated bodies, are antithetical to the buildings' historicist materials and design yet complement them. However, it is Sanders's Five Minute Bathroom (1999), commissioned by *Wallpaper* magazine—and made possible through digitally literate fabrication methods—that expands the notion of the leisure landscape to a complete spatial enclosure that reflects Ergotectonic principles.

Sanders designed the freestanding bathroom, made from prefabricated, molded fiberglass, to efficiently accommodate an "assembly line" of functions, from waking through dressing. The dressing closet, water closet, "smart mirror," and bed meld to form seamless spaces that gently fold into one another. While the Five Minute Bathroom seems reminiscent of R. Buckminster Fuller's design for his 1936 prototype 5 X 5 Bathroom Unit, Sanders takes Fuller's design one step further by incorporating the sleeping and dressing area to create a unit that can be installed in any location.

Traces of the Five Minute Bathroom are evident in Sanders's opulent Millennium residence (2001–2) in New York. In fact, this 1,300-square-foot renovation may represent the culmination of Ergotectonics. A single core volume, clad in acid-etched glass, is inserted into the footprint of the apartment, becoming the primary visual focus, main source of light, and organizing matrix. This core volume, its curvilinear interior lined in waterproof epoxy, represents a new iteration of Sanders's leisure landscape: it is conceived as a fully closed, fully occupiable shell, much like the Five Minute Bathroom. Surface transparency, opacity, and reflectivity allow the volume to reveal objects and silhouettes of objects contained within, from clothing to bodies. For example, a mirrored cabinet wall adjacent to the master suite (and visible from the living room) reflects the bed, rendering this very private domain a visually public space. Reflectivity and translucency (in the dressing closet, master shower, and elsewhere) both behave as visual tropes that speak to Sanders's rigorous questioning and subverting of the normative act of concealment.

The arrival of digital literacy in architecture has expanded the boundaries of the discipline to designs that can be fabricated directly from computer software by way of CNC milling machines. Sanders is one of the few architects who have explored the interior spatial ramifications feasible through digital production. As his work has become more digitally informed, his designs have come to possess a more fluid sense of interior space and exterior form. In the 24/7 Business Hotel (2002–3), a project commissioned for the exhibition "New Hotels for Global Nomads" at the Cooper-

Hewitt, National Design Museum, for instance, Sanders's leisure landscape is digitally morphed with his Five Minute Bathroom to create a compelling solution for the globe-trotting twenty-first-century traveler. The objective of the hotel is to retool the outmoded twelve-by-twenty-four-foot template of the traditional hotel room into an environment that is both pleasurable and productive. Sanders's solution recalls Le Corbusier's apartments for the Unité d'Habitation (1947–52) in Marseilles, France. Conceptually, in the case of Le Corbusier, and literally, for Sanders, individual units plug into a larger structural framework to generate the over-all building mass. Sanders's modular hotel concept can work at any economic level. His proposal for easyHotel (2003), a no-frills, clean-your-own-room residency fabri-cated from fiberglass components that can be joined to assume a variety of configurations, is a concept feasible only through digital production and mass customization.

While the twentieth-century steel-framed glass house has historically been the site for social spectacle and voyeurism, the twenty-first-century, digitally improved ver-sion of this dwelling typology has been inverted toward sur-veillance and safety. Sanders's Access House (2001–2) in Georgia addresses this dichotomy of spectacle and surveil-lance and best illustrates the evolution of his thinking about visuality since the Kyle residence. Designed as a vacation home for a retired couple and their extended family, the house consists of two interlocking folded forms wrapped in a glass skin and disposed to take advantage of the panoramic ocean views. This multilevel interior branches from what he calls the E:core—a physical and digital device centrally located and similar in concept to a telescope. Strategically placed sur-veillance cameras dispersed throughout the house and prop-erty transmit images to the E:core; these images can be observed via screens embedded into the surfaces of the inte-rior landscape or suspended from ceilings. Where the Kyle house relied on prescribed views, enclosures, and conceal-ment, the Access House is a visually open domestic pavilion (similar to the Farnsworth house) that inverts the notion of voyeurism, allowing the occupants to enjoy their own spec-tacle while at the same time surveilling others who might be viewing them. Ideologically, Sanders's E:core surveillance apparatus reconstitutes the spectacle of the Glass Pavilion as a viable domestic condition for the twenty-first century.

As Sanders's projects expand—from domestic to insti-tutional and civic—so does his methodology. This can be seen in his proposals for the expansion of the Fashion Institute of Technology (2003) and the Olympic Equestrian Facility (2003–), projects that mark a significant aesthetic shift in Sanders's work toward the employment of modu-lated patterned surfaces; such embellishment becomes a strategy that allows both designs to be highly contextual in terms of site and program.

Sanders's design for the FIT expansion developed a new patterned-glass cladding system based on the alternating geometrical pattern of the metal facade of an adjacent cam-pus building. The new, digitally fabricated, woven glass facade incorporates digital displays and acts as a billboard for the general public, detailing events taking place at the school.

The Olympic Equestrian Facility proposal, designed with Balmori Associates, is a masterful synthesis of pro-gram, context, and sustainability for the twenty-first cen-tury. The design brings disparate elements—stadium, press facilities, stables, and pedestrian bridge—into a cohesive assembly. Patterning appears once again, here in a series of benday dots, on the cladding of the structures as well as on the site itself, blurring the boundaries between buildings and landscape into a contiguous folding condition in a self-generated context. If these two recent proposals are any measure, Sanders's future prospects have the potential to generate a public architecture that, questioning conven-tional thinking, will lead to innovative spatial and social solutions—both Ergotectonic and digitally informed.

KYLE RESIDENCE HOUSTON, TEXAS, 1993

Our design for the Kyle residence takes as a point of departure the Farnsworth house by Mies van der Rohe. It reconsiders the modernist concept of transparency in the context of the contemporary American suburb. Unlike Mies's glass house, a solitary object set in an expansive rural setting, our project is sited on a constricted suburban plot surrounded by neighboring houses.

The design transforms the utility core of the Farnsworth house into a protective appliance wall that follows the setback lines of the site. From the outside, this high-tech fence establishes visual privacy. But when viewed from the interior, this opaque boundary dematerializes: the Astroturf roof, which shelters the master bedroom, and the reflective glass-enclosed lap pool seem to raise the level of the horizon, replacing unsightly views of neighboring properties with a series of constructed views of a synthetic "nature" in which lawn and water meet open sky.

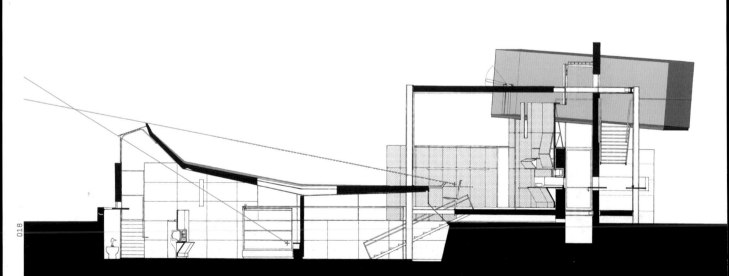

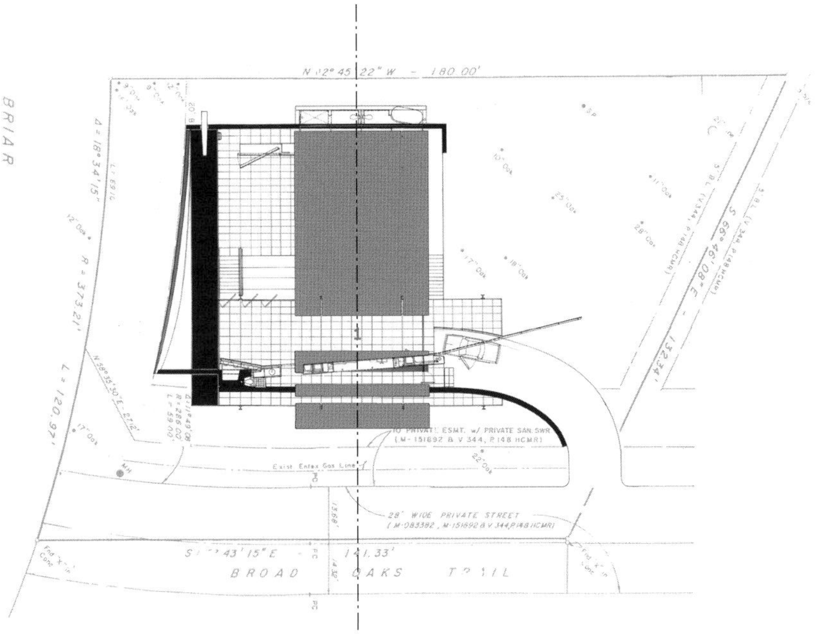
BRIAR
BROAD OAKS TRAIL
28' WIDE PRIVATE STREET
Exist Entex Gas Line

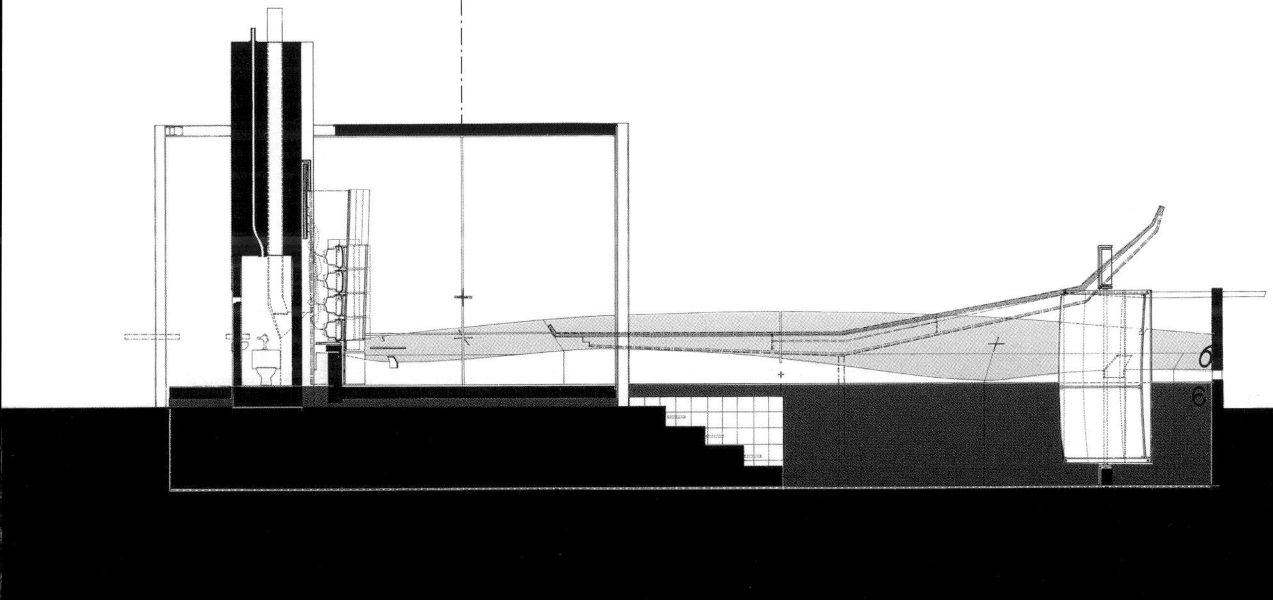

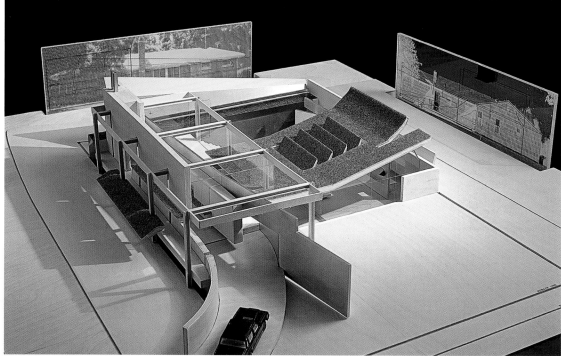

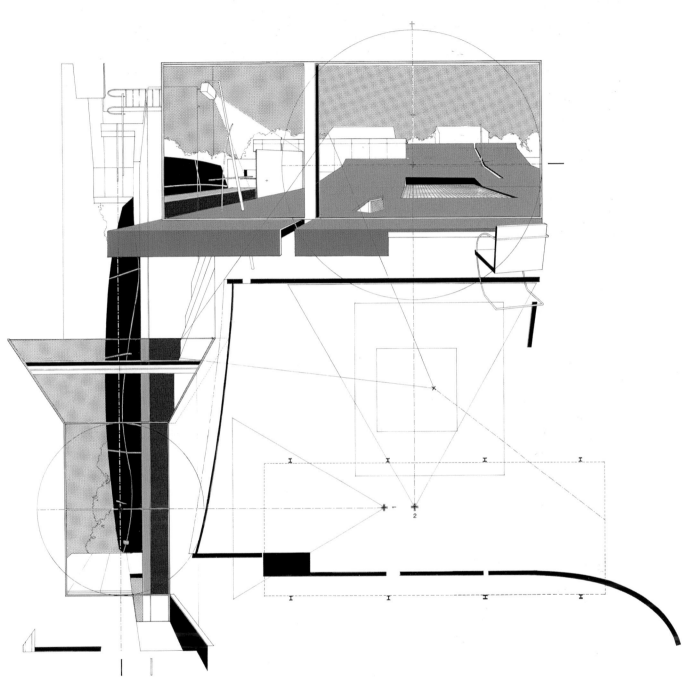

1

Good Fences, Good Neighbors

Neighboring properties disappear from the view from inside the house; the western and northern glass exposures frame constructed landscape views of water and lawn against the open horizon.

Sight Specific, commissioned for the exhibition "House Rules" at the Wexner Center for the Arts, reconfigures the plan of a typical developer home. An exterior space, or "front-backyard," replaces the interior space usually occupied by the infrequently used formal living and dining rooms. This new exterior area, a protected courtyard adjacent to the street, displaces the backyard to the front of the house, freeing up valuable floor area and enabling us to build two back-to-back houses on the same lot, thereby producing a hybrid urban-suburban condition. Like Siamese twins, these paired households are joined by a party wall that houses plumbing and HVAC.

We reorganized conventional visual relationships in an attempt to foster new social relationships, both between the house's occupants and between neighbors. The front facade resembles an oversized Venetian blind; its mechanical louvers allow inhabitants to regulate views to and from the street. Transparent and translucent apertures in the party wall facilitate scopic transparency without compromising privacy. The project features spatial as well as visual transgression of boundaries: part of the roof of one house penetrates the master bedroom of the other, creating a canopy over the conjugal bed. Paired lap pools overlap the two properties, allowing neighboring swimmers to share yards.

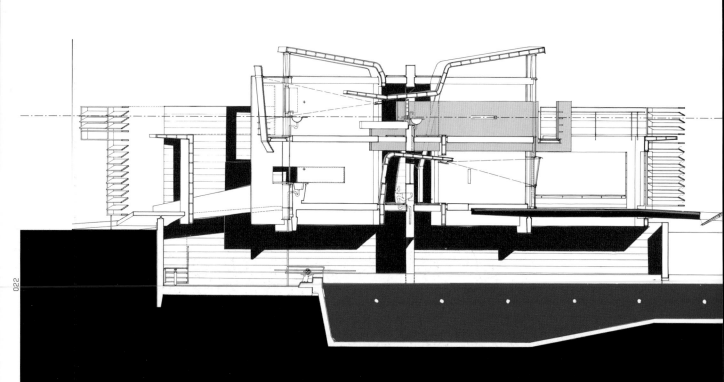

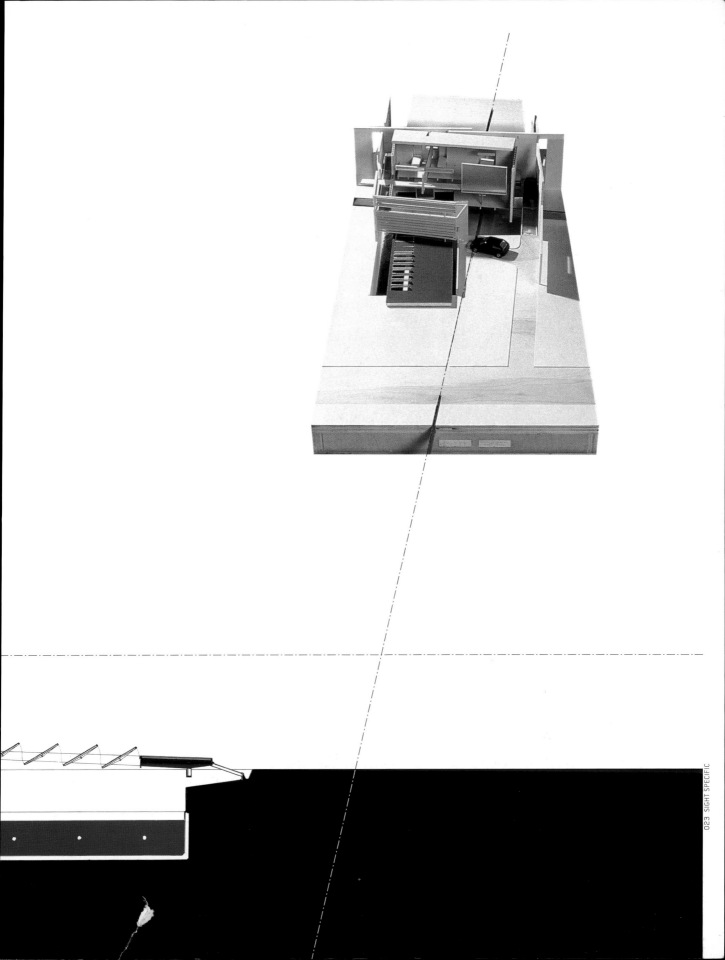

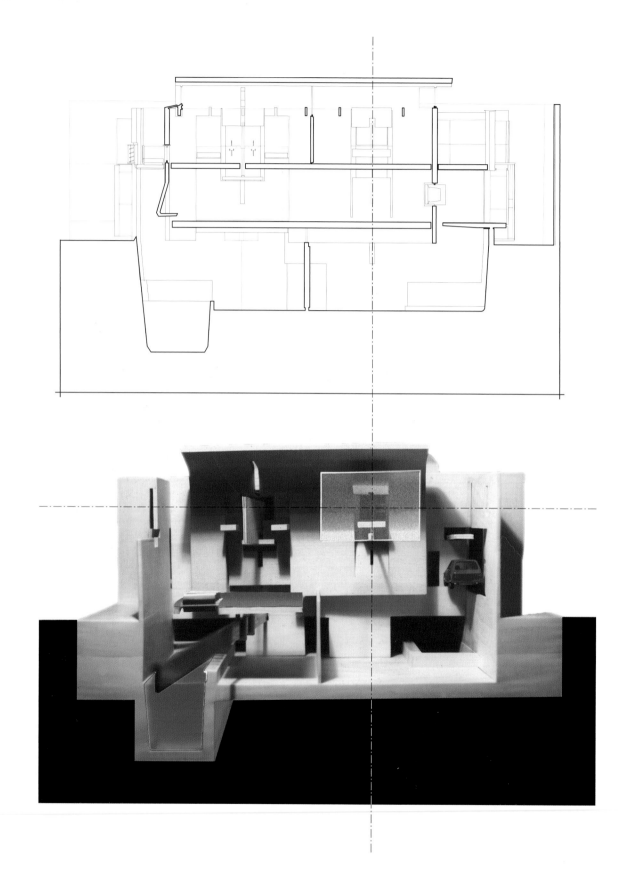

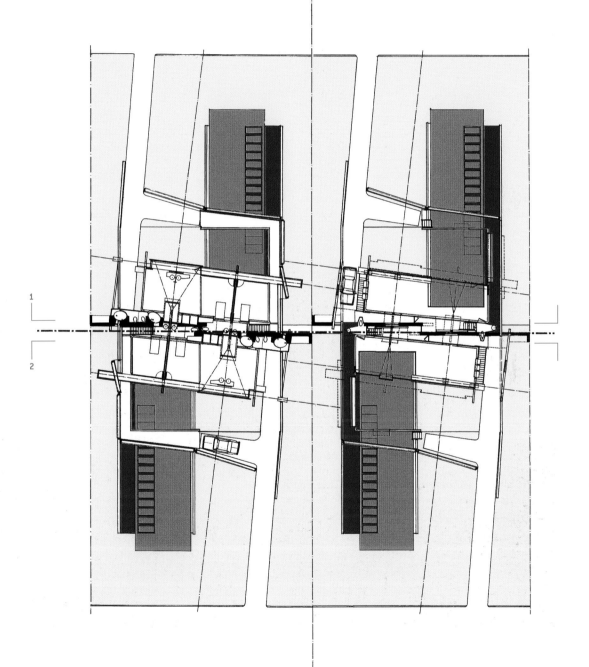

1

2

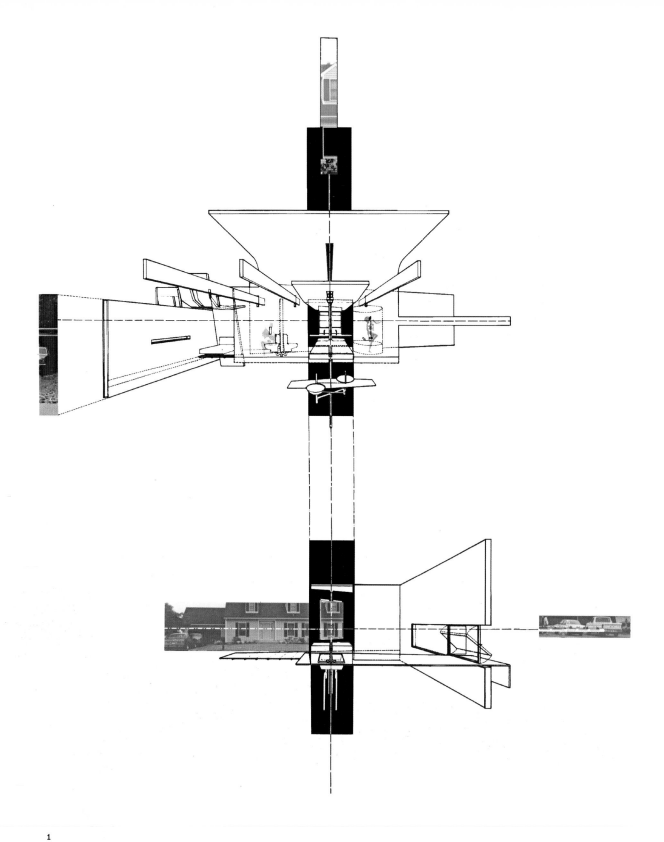

1

Sight Section North
A medicine chest in one house creates a window in the other, which permits the gaze to pass from the latter through the adjoining bedroom in the former and out to the street beyond.

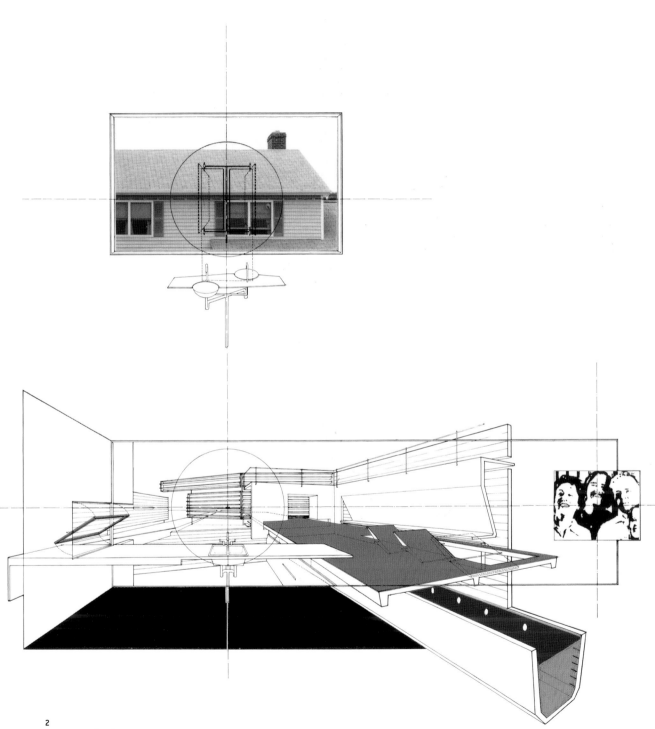

2
Sight Section South
While standing at the kitchen sink, occupants can survey the front-backyard and the street beyond through the louvered facade.

PEEKSKILL ARTISTS' LIVE-WORK HOUSING PEEKSKILL, NEW YORK, 1994–1996

In the early 1990s, in an effort to revitalize its declining downtown, Peekskill, New York, rezoned its commercial center to allow the construction of housing earmarked for artists. Located on a one-and-a-half-acre site, our project contains twenty-three live-work lofts; these residences redefine the relationship between the artist's studio and the domestic and public realms.

Unlike the traditional artist's loft—an open space that merges living and working—contemporary artist housing calls for studios that can both communicate with and be separate from the living quarters. Our project proposes a flexible membrane between live and work. Sliding doors and windows in this interior facade allow each artist to regulate visual, acoustic, and physical interaction between home and studio. Shadows of objects and human bodies are visible through the translucent plastic surface of the membrane, which at the top floor folds horizontally to become a north-facing skylight.

The linear mass of the building repairs the broken street wall of Central Avenue, a major downtown thoroughfare. A pedestrian path rings the perimeter of the building, activating the street as well as the stepped interior court that links the upper and lower levels of the steeply sloping site. Each studio is accessible from the public circulation route, thus doubling as a gallery. Shop windows facilitate the display of both people and objects.

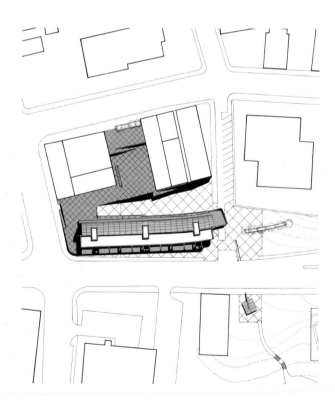

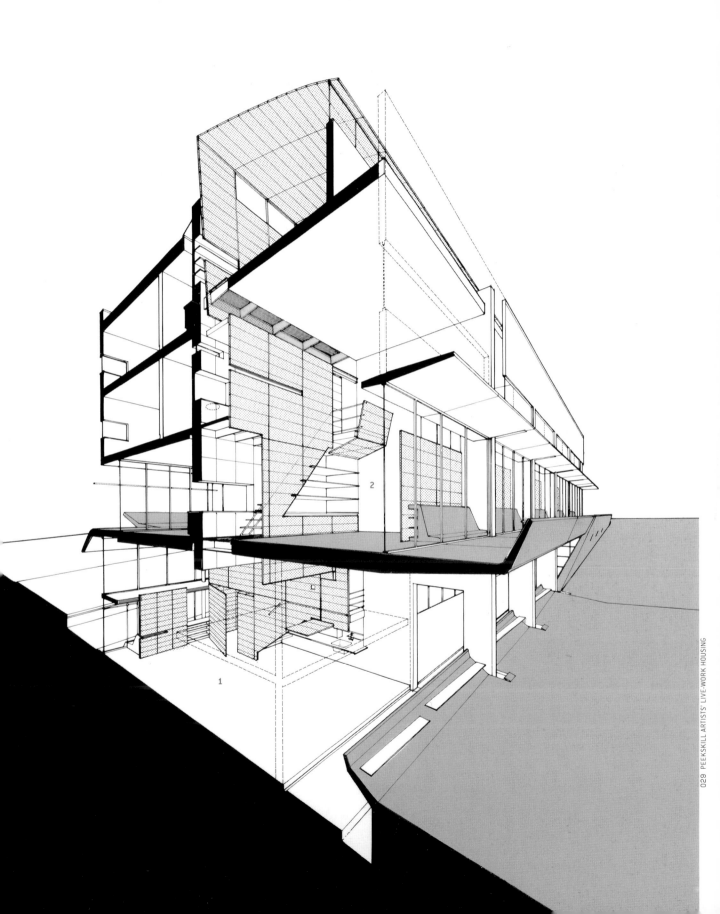

1

2

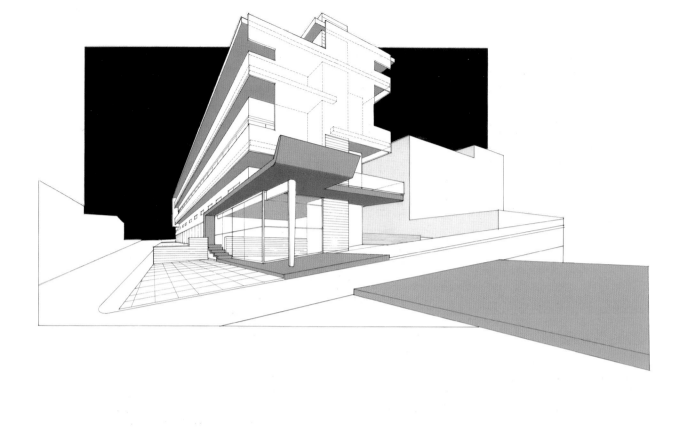

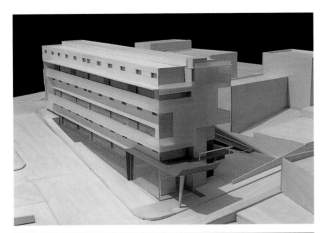

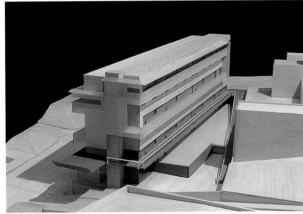

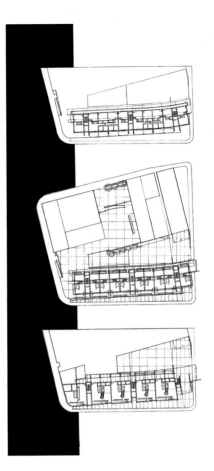

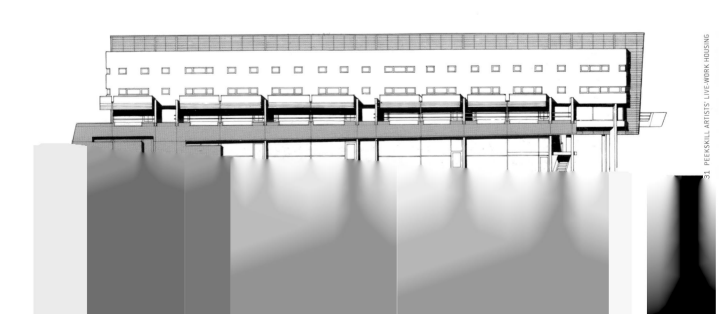

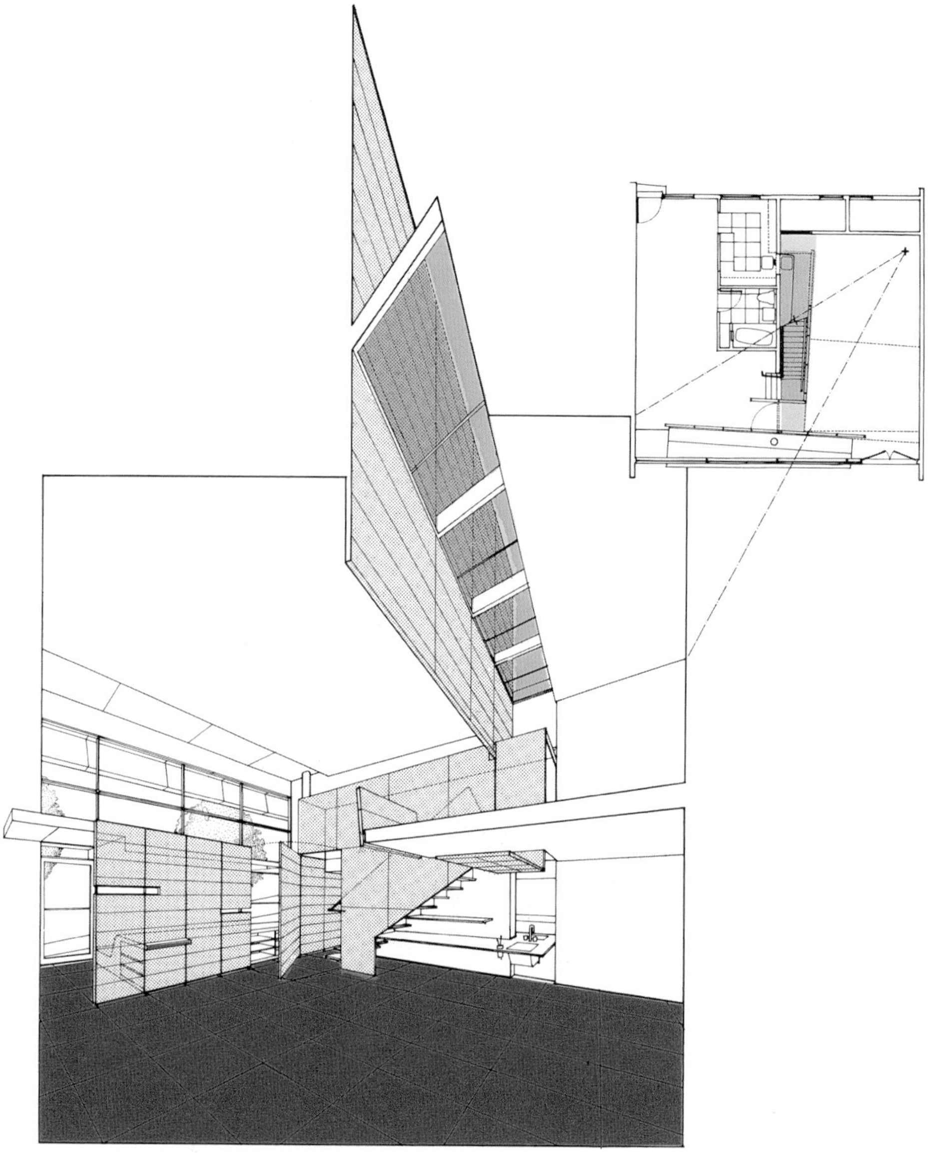

1

Plinth-Level Duplex

At street level, shop windows with translucent panels provide privacy and a backdrop for art when closed and allow the public to watch artists at work when open.

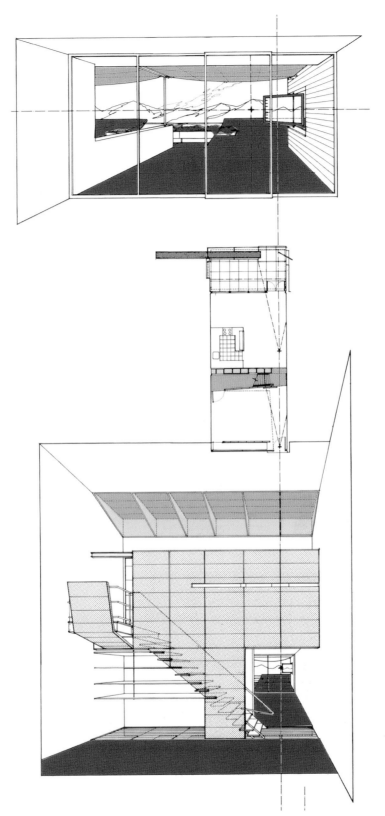

2
Upper-Level Unit
Operable panels in the translucent interior facade create apertures that allow the gaze to pass between studio, living quarters, and garden terrace.

ZIMENT ASSOCIATES NEW YORK, NEW YORK, 1996

The office we designed for Ziment Associates provides a flexible work environment for this market-research firm in a commercial loft in New York's Flatiron District. Our challenge was to differentiate private work space from the public areas reserved for clients and focus groups without compromising the sense of spatial continuity.

The layout ensures that every work station receives access to natural light and views to Fifth Avenue. The reception area and lounge block the windowed perimeter of the loft only when clients and focus groups arrive: a wall of manually operated steel-and-fiberglass pivoting screens can be closed to separate the lounge from the open office.

The expansive office area itself is defined by suspended ceiling panels with recessed task lighting. Three partition types define different activity zones. At the public entry, a white sheetrock wall punctured by a linear slit frames glimpses into the built-in work stations. The executive wing is defined by a birch plywood storage wall that contains files and establishes thresholds to private offices. Walls lined in cork tiles create back-to-back conference rooms: a large one for client presentations and focus groups and a smaller one equipped with pivoting doors that open directly into the main work area. Underscoring the guiding theme of multipurpose elements, the cork offers acoustical insulation as well as a tackable bulletin board.

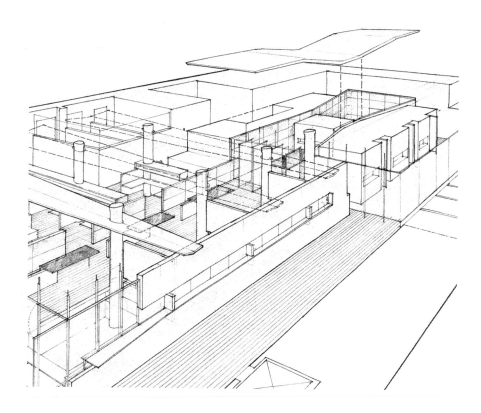

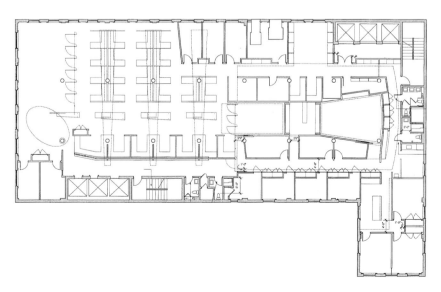

STUD: ARCHITECTURES OF MASCULINITY

In the opening passage of Ayn Rand's novel *The Fountainhead,* architect hero Howard Roark stands naked at the edge of a granite cliff surveying a panoramic view of a wooded valley below. *The Fountainhead* achieves its author's goal—"the presentation of an ideal man"[1]—by

1. Ayn Rand, *The Fountainhead* (1952; New York: Penguin Books, 1971), vii. Hereafter, all pages numbers are cited in the text.

portraying its male protagonist as an architect, capitalizing on the popular cultural perception that authors of buildings, like the structures they design, embody the very essence of manhood. Conflating the male architect's body with the landscape that elevates him, Rand's hard-edged prose lodges both masculinity and architecture in a transcendental natural world: "His face was like a law of nature— a thing one could not question, alter or implore" (15). Rand's description of Roark's robust physique, composed of "long, straight lines and angles, each curve broken into planes," seen silhouetted against the sky, recalls Frank Lloyd Wright's famous house Fallingwater, also a composition of hard geometric forms set against a rugged forest setting. An unfettered and independent creator with a single-minded concern for "the conquest of nature," the professional architect mines his intrinsic "manly" faculties; possessing both physical and mental prowess, Roark shapes and masters the natural forces that sustain him (679): "These rocks, he thought, are here for me: waiting for the drill, the dynamite and my voice; waiting to be split, ripped, pounded, reborn; waiting for the shape my hands will give them" (16). Rand's portrait of the architect as elemental man vividly dramatizes how culture relies upon architecture as a foundation for the construction of masculinity.

Architecture and masculinity, two apparently unrelated discursive practices, operate reciprocally in this remarkable opening scene from *The Fountainhead.* Rand exploits building metaphors to articulate the theme of "manworship," while the portrait of Howard Roark as creator sanctifies architectural doctrine. In the novel's central dramatic scene, the courtroom scene in which Roark is tried for dynamiting one of his own buildings "disfigured" during construction, Rand's uncompromising male idealist defends the principles of modern architecture with arguments comparing built structures to masculine virtue, claiming that buildings have integrity, just like men. Roark's narcissistic proclamation echoes the words of Western architects and theorists from Vitruvius to Le Corbusier who, in their attempt to locate and fix architecture's underlying principles in a vision of transhistorical nature, recruit masculinity to justify practice. Rand's architecture of masculinity offers one of the most dramatic, although certainly not the earliest, renditions of the notion that buildings derive from the human form itself—specifically from the unity, scale, and proportions of the male body.[2] *The Fountainhead*'s

2. For a discussion of how Renaissance architectural theorists (Alberti, Filarete, Di Giorgio) privilege the male body (excluding the female) in their discussions of the human form as architectural prototype, see Diana Agrest, "Architecture from Without: Body, Logic, and Sex" in her *Architecture from Without: Theoretical Framings for a Critical Practice* (Cambridge: MIT Press, 1991), 173–95.

portrayal of the architect as virile stud ultimately reveals architecture and masculinity to be mutually reinforcing ideologies, each invoking the other to naturalize and uphold its particular claims and intentions.[3]

3. Pursuing his ongoing interest in the reciprocity of architecture and philosophy, Mark Wigley traces "the relationships between the role of gender in the discourse of space and the role of space in the discourse of gender" in his essay "Untitled: The Housing of Gender," in *Sexuality and Space*, ed. Beatriz Colomina (New York: Princeton Architectural Press, 1992), 327–89, esp. 329.

In one of modern intellectual history's stranger alliances, contemporary cultural theorists have recently borrowed from architectural discourse the language of "construction" to *denaturalize* sexual identity. Arguing that identity is "constructed" rather than natural, "mapped" rather than given, these theorists draw on the popular perception of architecture as man-made precisely in order to de-essentialize gender. But in the process of erecting an argument about gender, cultural theory draws on a view of architecture—architecture as human artifice—that the discipline itself has, throughout its long history, sought either implicitly to camouflage or emphatically to deny.

Rarely are gender and architecture, allied and interdependent cultural productions, afforded the opportunity to address one another directly. *Stud* invites both theorists and architects, writers and artists, to expand the notion of cultural construction by investigating the active role that architectural constructions play in the making of gender. Through its mobilization of architectural metaphors to describe the "built" male body, Ayn Rand's *Fountainhead* illustrates one crucial way that culture enlists architecture to construct gender. But the same question can be broached from the opposite direction. How does architecture, as a concrete material practice, work to institute sexual identities by delimiting and demarcating the interaction of human subjects in actual space? While previous studies have tended to concentrate on architecture's role in the formation of feminine identities,[4] *Stud* questions how,

in the fabrication of masculine identities at specific sites and at precise moments in history.

Although engineering masculinity is a Herculean task, architecture never lets you see it sweat. Unless a building stands out as a monument with inscriptions incised in stone on its surface, we tend to forget that architecture is encumbered by politics and ideology. Normally, we regard edifices as neutral containers, facilitating the free interaction of sovereign subjects in space. But the ostensibly innocent conventions of architecture work in covert fashion to transmit social values in unexpected places—the everyday and often banal places where our daily lives unfold. Commonplace but ideologically overdetermined spaces—houses, bathrooms, gyms, offices, streets, parks—quietly and decisively participate in the manufacture of male subjectivity.

But how, exactly, does architecture work to construct gender identity through the distribution of bodies and objects in space? Recent critical theory offers us the suggestive notion of sexual identity as performance—as the compulsory repetition of culturally prescribed codes and utterances.[5] Architecture is one of the subjectivating norms

4. A partial list of significant works that examine architecture's impact on women from a feminist perspective includes Dolores Hayden, *The Grand Domestic Revolution: A History of Feminist Designs for American Homes, Neighborhoods and Cities* (Cambridge: MIT Press, 1981); Gwendolyn Wright, *Moralism and the Modern Home: Domestic Architecture and Cultural Conflict in Chicago, 1873–1913* (Chicago: University of Chicago Press, 1980); Susana Torre, *Women in American Architecture: A Historic and Contemporary Perspective* (New York: Whitney Library of Design, 1977); Leslie Kanes Weisman, *Discrimination By Design: A Feminist Critique of the Man-Made Environment* (Chicago: University of Illinois Press, 1994); Ellen Lupton and J. Abbott Miller, *The Bathroom, The Kitchen, and the Aesthetics of Waste: A Process of Elimination* (New York: Princeton Architectural Press, 1992); and Beatriz Colomina, ed., *Sexuality and Space* (New York: Princeton Architectural Press, 1992).

5. Drawing on the spatial metaphor of the theater, critics like Eve Kosofsky Sedgwick, Marjorie Garber, and Judith Butler all theorize gender as performance, useful for thinking about architecture as the space that supports and frames identity. Cautioning against thinking of gender as a choice made by a sovereign subject who freely fashions a self by performing a role, Judith Butler writes that "performativity is a matter of reiterating or repeating the norms by which one is constituted; it is not a radical fabrication of a gendered self. It is a compulsory repetition of prior and subjectivating norms, ones which cannot animate, and constrain of the gendered subject, and also the resources from which resistance, subversion, displacement are to be forged." See Butler, "Critically Queer," *GLQ* 1:1 (1993): 22.

through the careful organization and distribution of materials, objects, and bodies in space, physical structures assist

that constitute gender performativity. Programmatic functions in architecture are commonly associated with specific, although culturally contingent, spatial configurations, often referred to as building "types." For example, dwelling locates itself within the house, research within the library, working within the office—all formulaic structures made up of recurring formal elements offering relatively few variations. With rare exception, working within the spatial limits dictated by custom, and by a building industry driven by economic forces that encourage standardization, the architect or builder modifies a type in response to the particular pressures of a specific site or program. The moments in a design that do allow for the possibility of inflection and variation represent potential sites in architecture where norms and their attending ideologies can be reviewed, resisted, and revised. The way buildings distribute our activities within standard spatial configurations has a profound ideological impact on social interaction—regulating, constraining, and (on occasion) liberating the human subject. Architecture, through the establishment and the alteration of reiterated types and conventions, creates the space—the stage—where human subjectivity is enacted and performed.

What, then, are the formal codes and conventions that architecture deploys to erect masculinity, and where do they occur? Considering the problem at different scales— from the design of furniture and wall coverings to the layout of public parks—*Stud*'s contributors identify four architectural strategies that enhance male performance: dressing wall surfaces, demarcating boundaries, distributing objects, and organizing gazes.

DRESSING WALL SURFACES

The suggestion that architecture stages masculine performance through the treatment of interior and exterior wall surfaces contradicts one of the central tenets of architectural doctrine. By identifying manliness as "genuine" and womanliness as "artifice," architects since Vitruvius have associated the ornamented surface with femininity, not masculinity. Discussing the origins of Doric and Ionic columns, Vitruvius writes: "In the invention of the two different kinds of columns, they borrowed manly beauty, naked and unadorned, for the one, and for the other the

delicacy, adornment, and proportions characteristic of women."[6] Because of its long-standing associations with the

6. Vitruvius, *The Ten Books on Architecture*, trans. Morris Hicky Morgan (New York: Dover, 1960), 104.

feminine, ornament came under sustained attack in the twentieth century from architectural modernists invested in upholding the notion of a building's pared-down inner truth.[7] Searching for an authentic, rational, and timeless

7. See Mary McLeod, "Undressing Architecture: Fashion, Gender, and Modernity," and Mark Wigley, "White Out: Fashioning the Modern," both in *Architecture: In Fashion*, ed. Deborah Fausch et al. (New York: Princeton Architectural Press, 1994), 38–123 and 148–268.

architecture, Le Corbusier and others have found their archetypal model in the image of the male nude ("naked and unadorned," like Ayn Rand's architect hero) rather than in the picture of the female masquerader, embellished with clothes and makeup. But while the image of the male nude was seen to embody masculine ideals of rationality and strength, the functional imperative that requires buildings to wear a protective outer skin implicitly challenged modernism's devaluation of ornament. As Mark Wigley notes, Le Corbusier's "Law of Ripolin"—the thin coat of whitewash painted on the pristine walls of modern buildings and associated with such masculine traits as logic, hygiene, and truth—functions, despite its apparent invisibility, as an applied layer, a form of clothing added to the surface of buildings.[8] Recognizing the practical indispensability of

8. Wigley, "White Out."

this second skin for dressing the building surface, Adolf Loos recommends that designers emulate the timeless simplicity of the austere, standardized wardrobe of an Englishman. Both examples suggest that masculinity, no less than femininity, is constructed through the use of supplemental surfaces.

Even the materials employed to construct buildings are implicated in a process of architectural gendering. Coded as ruggedly masculine, wood paneling is conventionally used for sheathing recreational and professional interiors (men's clubs, bars, law courts, corporate boardrooms). The hard, cold, crystalline surfaces of building materials such as glass, steel, and stone are similarly attributed masculine properties. Often these materials evoke the "manly" environments that produced them: wood conjures up a vision of a preindustrialized, predomesticated masculine wilderness, while steel invokes a picture of virile laborers shaping molten metals in foundries. Le Corbusier derived his lexicon of materials from building types mainly inhabited by men (factories and monasteries) as well as from the traditionally male domain of transportation (cars, ships, airplanes). But while these materials directly recall male environments, they also more subtly convey the social values associated with them. A building's architectural integrity derives from the masculinization of its materials, which are made to bear the weight of the cultural values masculinity purportedly connotes, above all austerity, authenticity, and permanence. Ironically, architects value the supplemental skins used to register masculinity precisely because of their innate, hence "manly," characteristics. Electing to forego the use of applied ornament, architects like Mies van der Rohe (at the Barcelona Pavilion) and Adolf Loos (at the American Bar, Vienna) favored wood and marble, materials prized for their inherent natural patterns.

Two exclusively male domiciles invite us to see through the masculine garb of modern architecture. *Playboy*'s Penthouse Apartment for a Bachelor by an unidentified designer (1956) and the Air Force Academy at Colorado Springs by Skidmore, Owings & Merrill (1958) each reveal, in their respective attempts to showcase masculine austerity, an almost obsessive concern with style.[9] Eschewing the upholstered furniture and applied

9. For a detailed discussion of the design of Skidmore, Owings & Merrill's military complex, see *Modernism at Mid-Century: The Architecture of the Air Force Academy*, ed. Robert Bruegmann (Chicago: University of Chicago Press, 1994).

fabrics and wallpapers that conventionally define a feminine interior, the designs for both the *Playboy* apartment and the Air Force Academy show single-sex environments tacitly organized for the performance and display of masculine power. *Playboy*'s "handsome haven" places stylish pieces of designer furniture made of steel, leather, and wood—a Florence Knoll desk, an Eames lounge chair, a Noguchi coffee table—within spaces defined by wood and glass partitions. The Air Force Academy interiors and furnishings, created by Walter Dorwin Teague Associates,

use similar materials (dark wood paneling and aluminum-framed furniture) to create orderly and highly regimented living quarters, places where cadets train to become men. The exhibitionist overtones of even the most spartan masculine spaces are particularly striking at the Air Force Academy, where built-in wood closets, opened daily for inspections, reveal military uniforms custom-designed by Hollywood director and designer Cecil B. DeMille. Framed within the closets and hung in a series prescribed by military protocol, these uniforms reinforce the

image of masculine regimentation, hierarchy, and control symbolized by the outfits themselves. The Air Force Academy closets demonstrate how the wall dressings that adorn a building work analogously to the clothes that outfit a body. But more often than not, architecture fabricates a masculine environment by undressing rather than dressing its surfaces: less is more masculine. Thus the campus plan of the Air Force Academy illustrates how masculine space is created by reducing architecture to its bare essentials. Each academy building, whose design is generated from a seven-foot grid derived from the module of a cadet's bed, is set on a vast, barren horizontal podium that levels the rugged topography to afford an uninterrupted view of the horizon. These empty plazas create an atmosphere as spare and forbidding as the bare Rocky Mountain range that serves as their imposing backdrop. The building interiors are also conspicuously lacking in detail, conveying the same virtues of cleanliness, order, and restraint connoted by the academy's spartan exteriors.

Artists Andrea Zittel and John Lindell also fabricate austere manly environments, employing a severe aesthetic associated with the rational languages of modern architecture and minimalist art. Zittel's "A to Z" lexicon of domestic prototypes consists of reductive geometric objects that accommodate and contain household functions—eating,

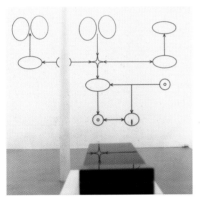

sleeping, bathing—within a minimal, often collapsible space. While Zittel's proposals for contemporary spartan living would seem to situate her within the masculinist tradition of the heroic modern architect, confident in his abilities to forge a rational world through the creation of standardized artifacts that obey universal human needs, her status as a contemporary female artist makes it ambiguous whether Zittel intends her interpretation of modernist austerity to be read as prescription, parody, or critique. Lindell's installations both celebrate and subvert the masculine visual codes he appropriates. In *Untitled*, Lindell uses his signature template of abstract symbols denoting male

erogenous zones to overturn the logic of the flow-chart diagrams commonly used by natural and social scientists to represent the steps of rational processes and procedures. Conflating the language of science and that of geometric abstraction, the crisp black lines and abstract shapes that Lindell draws on pristine white gallery walls map activities that fall outside the binary logic of heterosexuality—representing instead the ecstatic, even delirious geometries of gay male pleasure. Both Zittel's and Lindell's projects underscore how the articulation of masculine space often obeys a logic of absence—a logic implicitly predicated on the eradication of "feminine" excess or ornamentation.

Renee Green's *Commemorative Toile Fabric* calls into question the traditional association of ornamentation and femininity by demonstrating how ostensibly feminine surfaces of toile fabric historically embody masculine civic virtue. A commodity traded by French merchants in exchange for slaves, eighteenth-century toile fabric featured idyllic pastoral scenes representing an Enlightenment idealization of untamed nature. Exposing the violence of the sexual and racial economies that supported the trade in toile fabric, Green's contemporary designs for this material seamlessly splice together engraved scenes of rape, abduction, lynching, and slavery. By showing, through her visual alterations, how a material as supposedly neutral as toile fabric can encode dominant cultural ideologies, Green reminds us that the female domestic interior is not opposed to but is wholly complicit with the politics of the male public sphere.

DEMARCATING BOUNDARIES

This opposition of public and private, upon which sexual binaries like male/female and heterosexual/homosexual depend, is itself grounded in a prior spatial dualism, inside/outside.[10] Through the erection of partitions

10. For more on the spatial metaphorics of sexual identity, see Diana Fuss's introduction to *Inside/Out: Lesbian Theories, Gay Theories*, ed. Diana Fuss (New York and London: Routledge, 1991), 1–10.

that divide space, architecture colludes in creating and upholding prevailing social hierarchies and distinctions. Working on vastly different scales—from developer house plans that sequester the housewife in the kitchen from the husband in the family room to large-scale urban master plans that isolate the feminine world of the suburb from the masculine world of the city—architectural boundaries like walls and partitions have traditionally reconsolidated cultural gender differences by monitoring the flow of people and the distribution of objects in space.

The spatial differentiation of the sexes may find its most culturally visible form in the construction of the sexually segregated public bathroom. It is not by accident that Jacques Lacan chooses, as his privileged example of the institutionalization of sexual difference, adjoining public bathrooms in a railway station. Seated opposite one another by the window of a train pulling into a station, a boy and a girl misrecognize their socially prescribed destinations. "Look," says the brother. "We're at Ladies!" "Idiot!" replies his sister. "Can't you see we're at Gentlemen?"[11]

11. Jacques Lacan, *Écrits: A Selection*, trans. Alan Sheridan (New York: W. W. Norton, 1977), 153.

In this parable of what he calls the "laws of urinary segregation," Lacan attributes the division of sexes to the powerful signifying effects of language. But sexual difference here is also a function of spatial division. Lacan's reduction of the problem of sexual difference to the two-dimensional surface of a pair of bathroom doors conceals the more complex ways that the actual three-dimensional space of the public bathroom assigns sex and gender identity. The architecture of the public bathroom, where physical walls literally segregate the sexes, naturalizes gender by separating "men" and "women" according to the biology of bodily functions.

While Lacan shows us two bathroom doors identical in every respect but their labels, we never see beyond to the interiors themselves, which in fact are quite different. The common assumption that purely functional requirements specified by anatomical difference dictate the spatial layout and fixture design of rest-room architecture reinforces the reigning essentialist notion of sexual identity as an effect of biology. Just one look inside the typical domestic bathroom shared by both sexes discloses the ways in which segregated public rest-room facilities answer to the requirements of culture, not nature.

Two public bathroom renovations, one by Interim Office of Architecture and the other by Sheila Kennedy and Frano Violich, emphasize the contingent status of a cultural site generally considered functionally fixed and inevitable. In renovations at two urban art centers, these design teams attempt to make visible the architectural codes of the bathroom that shape and regulate sexual identity. In the modernization of the Boston Arts Center, a nineteenth-century exhibition hall, Kennedy and Violich invert conventional gender assignments by placing the building's new women's room where the men's room used to be and vice versa. Bruce Tomb and John Randolph of IOOA reconfigure the laws of urinary segregation by converting the bathroom at the Headlands in San Francisco, once a single-sex military latrine, into a coed public lavatory. Each design team exposes architectural traces normally concealed in renovations. A row of freestanding "dysfunctional" urinals at the Headlands and a row of urinal floor drains left beneath newly installed sinks in the women's room at the Boston Arts Center are intrusive reminders of the culturally encoded urinary postures enforced by the architectural practices that govern sexual difference.

The men's room appears to function as a cultural space that consolidates masculine authority around the centrality of phallic power. But as Lee Edelman suggests in *Stud*'s section on the bathroom, this particular hygienic site also operates as a theater of heterosexual anxiety. Edelman argues that the anus, an orifice open to penetration, must be closeted in a stall to protect against the "homophobically abjectified desires" provoked by the "loosening of the sphincter." The internal spatial boundary within the men's room that separates the urinals from the enclosed toilets, together with the cultural prohibition against looking at one's neighbor while urinating, actually initiates what the structure of the men's room was meant to ward off: fear of the abject and homosexual desire. Edelman's discussion of a chic New York restaurant's men's room, where televisions are installed over the urinals to fix wandering glances, reflects the capacity of architecture to participate in the formation of heterosexual identity by giving cultural play to the forbidden and threatening desires its spatialized boundaries purportedly labor to conceal. In the overdetermined site of the public men's room, the door apparently swings both ways.

Philippe Starck's designs for public bathrooms effectively challenge the conventions of men's room architecture, highlighting and encouraging those activities and desires that standard ones suppress. While facilities for urinating and defecating are normally discreetly placed opposite one another, at the Royalton Hotel in Manhattan they share a common wall: the urinal, in the form of a vertical steel plane, is situated between flanking cubicle doors. Registering the movements of both eye and body, the urinal's metallic surface reflects wandering glances while a motion detector, activated by unzipping flies, initiates the flow of a sheet of water down its face. Further rejecting the norm of the isolated bathroom fixture, which insures an individual's sense of hygiene and propriety, at both the Royalton and the Teatriz in Madrid, Starck creates communal sinks that make washing a public activity as well.

A number of the projects in *Stud* highlight the ideological instability of the partition ordinarily found in toilets, gyms, peep shows, and sex clubs. Translucent dividers counteract the visual privacy afforded by Kennedy and Violich's rest-room stalls, while flexible plumbing hoses shake when flushed in IOOA's bathroom restoration, immediately undermining the authority of the undulating quarter-inch steel privacy screen rendered tough as military armor. Looking at this contentious membrane from an explicitly queer perspective, media critic Bill Horrigan's essay, which introduces architect Mark Robbins's project "Framing American Cities," shows how the cubicle refers not only to toilet stalls but also to peep shows and confessionals. Robbins's installation demonstrates how this vulnerable, penetrable boundary, originally designed as a spatial bulwark against the threat of homosexual predation, actually serves as an eroticized site of gay male sexual coupling.

DISTRIBUTING OBJECTS

Within the spaces articulated by the enclosing boundaries of architecture, any performance of masculinity requires its props. A number of the contributions to this volume consider the obsessive, even hysterical ways that men relate to the objects that surround and define them. Men's overestimation of certain fetish objects points to the vulnerability at the very heart of masculine identity, a phenomenon that cultural critics, writing from a variety of perspectives, have described as masculinity in crisis. Some historians attribute the precarious nature of maleness to specific historical events—the industrial revolution, World War II—that transformed traditional roles both in the workplace and in the home. Psychoanalysts attribute the rents in male subjectivity to the formation of sexual identity itself, where the biological penis can never live up to the mystique of the cultural phallus.[12] In both readings, objects locate and reconfig-

12. For historical explanations of the modern crisis in masculinity, see Michael S. Kimmel, "Consuming Manhood: The Feminization of American Culture and the Recreation of the Male Body, 1832–1920," in *The Male Body: Features, Destinies, Exposures,* ed. Lawrence Goldstein (Ann Arbor: University of Michigan Press, 1994), 12–41, and Anthony Rotundo, *American Manhood: Transformations in Masculinity from the Revolution to the Modern Era* (New York: Basic Books, 1993). For a psychoanalytic reading of masculinity as masquerade, see Kaja Silverman, *Male Subjectivity at the Margins* (New York and London: Routledge, 1992).

ure masculine identity in historically specific and psychologically powerful ways.

The urinal itself is just such a culturally weighted sign, a brace for the erection and support of male subjectivity. By facilitating the manly posture of upright urination, the urinal illustrates the capacity of objects to function as foils against which a performing body assumes its gender. But objects not only supplement the body, they metaphorically stand in for it. In the famous cabaret scene of the film *Blue Angel,* Marlene Dietrich's long legs and lithe torso pose seductively against the contours of a Thonet chair, theatricalizing a feminine identity in contradistinction to her masculine attire. In itself a gender-neutral object, the Thonet chair behaves almost like a human partner, providing a prop for the interactive articulation of sexual identity. Shown in this volume, Robert Gober's urinals emphasize the anthropomorphic qualities

of architectural objects in much the same way as Dietrich's chair. Acting like surrogate males, their protruding profiles suggest a cross section through the male body. But unlike the polished, mass-produced, machine-made urinals with dimensions derived from the standard of an ideal male, Gober's handmade plaster urinals impersonate masculine vulnerability. Gober's urinals present

emblems of an ideal but unrealizable masculinity, vacillating uneasily between power and privilege on the one hand and failure and insufficiency on the other.

Steven Cohan attributes Rock Hudson's success as a playboy in the 1959 film *Pillow Talk* to his impressive equipment: his modern telephone, hi-fi, and electronically operated sofa bed all function as technological sex aids that compensate for, while nonetheless accentuating, Hudson's fragile virility. And Ellen Lupton describes how another postwar domestic gadget, the electric carving knife, was designed to bolster the insecure ego of America's new suburban husband. The electric knife, a household appliance originally marketed for women, was eventually adopted by men as a device that allowed them to perform the traditional male ritual of meat carving with greater prowess and confidence. However, in rendering simple a task that once required artistry, strength, and skill, this mechanical prosthesis also functioned as a powerful reminder of the social castration of the American male. Thus, in both authors' accounts, mechanical objects designed to proclaim phallic mastery disguise a deeper anxiety, just as Americans struggled to shore up a stable masculine identity against the emasculating effects of postwar consumer culture and the corporate workplace.

While domestic prosthetics compensate for the suburban male's imagined sense of his lost virility, at Rem Koolhaas's Maison à Bordeaux a mechanical device enables its owner—a man confined to a wheelchair—to overcome his actual loss of physical mobility. Ironically, here it is the husband rather than the housewife who needs to be liberated from the "prison" of the traditional home. But while buildings for the physically challenged typically avoid level changes, this design welcomes the challenge posed by its mountainside setting. The project consists of three stacked "houses" intersected by a hydraulic lift—a moving room that allows the husband to circulate freely between floors.

Its status literally elevated by the lift, the wheelchair, once an index of its owner's vulnerability, comes to confer power. A storage wall adjacent to the lift vertically penetrates the house, providing the husband with easy access to his possessions—books, artworks, wine—and allowing him to cultivate his worldly pursuits. From the vantage point of his moving perch, floor-to-ceiling windows on the second level afford unobstructed panoramic views. The prosthetic architecture of Koolhaas's Maison restores to its owner visual and physical freedom, attributes necessary for the successful performance of masculinity.

Artist Matthew Barney takes this consideration of masculine performativity as the overcoming of physical obstacles even further, unveiling masculinity as an overt challenge—a trial performed under constant pressure and anxiety. Barney's *OTTOshaft,* an installation mounted in a concrete parking garage at Documenta IX, investigates how

the mainstays of masculinity present literal obstacles to the achievement of gender identity. The installation's meticulously crafted objects (exercise mats covered in tapioca, blocking sleds used in football training lathered in petroleum jelly, collapsed gym lockers made of pink plastic typically used for prosthetic devices) define masculinity in relation to sports, sex, and metabolic functions. Using these objects as performance props, Barney enacts a variety of masculine roles for the videos that he both shoots and displays within the installation space itself. The videos show us Barney, wearing only a harness, subjecting his naked flesh to an excruciating and bizarre set of physical endurance tests. Scaling an elevator shaft, dropping from the ceiling, and even submitting to anal probes, Barney's contemporary rite of heroic

self-fashioning parodies what it seeks to impersonate, intentionally implicating himself, in his role as male performance artist, in the very rituals of masculine display he aims to unmask.

ORGANIZING GAZES

Architecture regulates subjectivity not only through the arrangement of objects in particular spatial structures but also through the organization of spectatorship within those same spaces. From panoptic prisons to pornographic theaters, numerous building types endow men with visual authority while regulating disempowered subjects—especially women—to the position of scopophilic objects. But while visual control remains a recurrent theme in the architectural construction of masculinity, in many circumstances the spatial distribution of the gaze undermines men's culturally privileged access to vision. Several of the pieces in this volume demonstrate how specific architectural spaces work to destabilize the active/passive, subject/object, male/female binaries upon which conventional theories of spectatorship depend. This disturbance of the gaze works in at least two ways: masculine subjects endowed with visual authority can be dispossessed of the gaze through changing configurations of spatial boundaries; even the most traditional masculine environments are capable of encouraging a transvestite logic of viewing, inviting men to be both subjects and objects of the gaze.[13]

13. A significant body of work in contemporary film theory examines the notion of male spectacle and its potentially destabilizing effects for regimes of spectatorship. See, for example, Richard Dyer's "Don't Look Now: The Male Pin-Up" and Steve Neale's "Masculinity as Spectacle," both in *The Sexual Subject: A Screen Reader in Sexuality* (New York and London: Routledge, 1992), 265–76 and 277–87. The classic analysis of the gender politics of spectatorship can be found in Laura Mulvey's "Visual Pleasure and Narrative Cinema" in her *Visual and Other Pleasures* (Bloomington: Indiana University Press, 1989), 14–26.

The essay by Diana Fuss and myself takes up the first of these possibilities, mapping the visual organization of Sigmund Freud's Vienna office to explore the complicated play of power and transference at work within the spatial and historic scene of psychoanalysis. This essay calls into question the traditional view of Freud's professional office as a space of male dominion, one in which patients are rendered powerless in the face of the analyst's absolute scopic authority. The actual architectural configuration of

Freud's office and the arrangement of furniture and objects within it suggest a far more complicated dynamic between patient and doctor, a scenario in which Freud more often than not adopts a passive position while his patient is permitted to occupy the room's center of activity. In the highly mediated settings of both his study and his consulting room, Freud assumes a spatially marginalized position, one that leaves him perpetually vulnerable to the risk of feminization.

Focusing on a very different kind of cultural arena, one perhaps more obviously overdetermined as a site of masculine performance, Marcia Ian analyzes the gym as a socially sanctioned space where men become the object of the gaze. The success of the male bodybuilder who pumps iron to "substitute the rock hard for the soft, the monumental for the human, and the masculine for the feminine" is registered through the visual admiration of his fellow bodybuilders. Within the confines of the gym, whose mirrored surfaces disperse the gaze in many directions, men willingly submit to a process of scopophilic objectification, readily assuming a receptive position so that they might ultimately attain physical supremacy.

The homoerotic possibilities of the gym point to the role of architecture in the formation of the modern sexual subject. The architectonics of gay male sexuality take place across an urban landscape of streets and parks, sex clubs and theaters, bathrooms and bars. Queer theorists have demonstrated how normative architectural spaces are recoded and remapped, a process that often involves shoring up a vulnerable straight masculinity by disavowing the specter of gay sexuality. Arguing against any essentialist notion of "queer space," *Stud*'s contributors demonstrate instead the many inventive and resourceful ways men have appropriated everyday public domains in the formation of a gay social identity.

Overturning the assumption that urban queer visibility commences with Stonewall, George Chauncey investigates the many ways in which the public spaces of cities have been claimed, in the past, by the gay community. His research on New York City's homosexual underground from 1890 to 1940 demonstrates that gay men have annexed and recodified as venues for social interaction and sexual desire a wide variety of urban spaces, including bars, streets, beaches, and parks.

The diverse physical characteristics of queer spaces resist categorization. Although gays stereotypically congregate in dark, deserted sites at the fringes of the city, like abandoned piers and overgrown parks, they just as often make contact in busy open streets. Yet a common feature with significant spatial implications belongs to all of these divergent spaces—the central importance of the gaze. D. A. Miller has written, "Perhaps the most salient index to male homosexuality, socially speaking, consists precisely in how a man looks at other men."[14] Constantly

14. David Miller, "Anal Rope," in Fuss, *Inside/Out,* 131.

subject to the threat of public and private surveillance, gay men have invented strategies for remaining invisible to the public while at the same time, and in the same spaces, becoming visible or readily identifiable to one another. For this reason, queers have had to depend not only on legible signs—clothing, grooming, mannerisms—but on the visibility of the look itself to identify other queers.[15] In his

15. Ironically, at the same time that gay men have had to rely on visual codes in the formation of countercultural space, they have had to evade the punitive gaze of mainstream culture, which has endeavored to render visibly discernible the always ambiguous face of the gay male. Lee Edelman describes how the dominant order, in its frustrated efforts to police the homosexual whose threatening presence risks exposing the unstable foundations of heterosexuality, had attempted to denaturalize the gay male body and scrutinize it for signs of its difference from "authentic" heterosexual maleness. See Edelman's "Imagining the Homosexual: Laura and the Other Face of Gender," in his *Homographesis: Essays in Gay Literary and Cultural Theory* (New York and London: Routledge, 1994), 192–241.

important study *Tearoom Trade: Impersonal Sex in Public Spaces,* sociologist Laud Humphreys has shown how communication through eye contact governs the carefully staged choreography of cruising.[16] His study documents

16. Laud Humphreys, *Tearoom Trade: Impersonal Sex in Public Places* (New York: Aldine De Gruyter, 1970).

how the precise layout of rest-room architecture—the location and number of urinals in relation to the placement of stalls—shapes the relay of desiring gazes that signals each player's shifting but precisely defined role in sexual encounters. Humphreys emphasizes that the carnal pleasures initiated by visual exchanges presuppose spaces capable of monitoring and surveillance: open or broken windows and squeaking doors permit the vigilant lookout to detect hostile intruders.

Tom Burr's historical reconstruction of Platzspitz Park in Zurich clarifies not only that the space of desire is also the space of surveillance but that spaces appropriated by socially dispossessed groups can be reappropriated through public renovation. Burr re-creates the Platzspitz Park as it appeared in the 1970s, when its secluded enclaves and dimly lit paths provided fertile terrain for the emergence of a gay urban space. His account describes how gays actively altered the spaces they annexed, intro-

ducing hidden paths and sheltered areas made readable to the initiated by deposits of litter and forgotten clothing. Burr's full-scale mock-up of the Platzspitz's design, displayed in the Landesmuseum overlooking the park itself, stands in stark contrast to the park's current landscape, which features well-lighted sweeping vistas and open spaces. These dramatic renovations, introduced to maximize visibility, also eradicate the presence of the very community that had previously so successfully carved out its own private sanctuary in the park.

Queer appropriations of the gaze undermine normative codes of spectatorship by creating a reversible look that allows a man to be both spectator and spectacle. The architecture of queer visibility troubles the heterosexist assumptions behind the look by overturning the social interdictions forbidding male spectacle.[17] Steven Barker's hidden camera

17. Patriarchal spectatorship is predicated on the strict division between identification and desire. Conventionally, men, as bearers of the active look, are prohibited from identifying with women, the passive objects of their desire, because to be seen is to be emasculated, castrated by a sadistic male gaze. Jacques Lacan describes the castrating power of the exteriorized gaze in *The Four Fundamental Concepts of Psychoanalysis*, trans. Alan Sheridan (New York: Norton, 1978).

documents a recently closed sex club that occupied a former movie theater. Previously, the building's proscenium arch focused the unidirectional gaze of the audience on a discretely framed moving image. Now, the gay men who occupy the theater and engage in openly visible sex acts consent to see and be seen, thereby blurring the boundary between spectator and spectacle, voyeur and exhibitionist.

The issue of the gaze underscores the way in which all human inhabitants of space, regardless of their gender identity, assume, to varying degrees, reversible and fluctuating positions, a condition that patriarchal society considers threatening. Taken together, *Stud*'s essays and projects collectively call our attention to the always unstable and fluid nature of human identities transacted through space.

ADAPTED FROM *STUD: ARCHITECTURES OF MASCULINITY,* ED. JOEL SANDERS (NEW YORK: PRINCETON ARCHITECTURAL PRESS, 1996).

BERGGASSE 19: INSIDE FREUD'S OFFICE (WITH DIANA FUSS)

In May 1938, on the eve of Sigmund Freud's expulsion from Vienna and flight to London, Freud's colleague August Aichhorn met with the photojournalist Edmund Engelman at the Café Museum on Karlsplatz to make a proposal. Would it be possible, Aichhorn wondered, to take photographs of Freud's office and apartment without drawing the attention of the Gestapo who, since Hitler's annexation of Austria two months earlier, had been keeping the home of one of Vienna's most famous Jewish intellectuals under constant surveillance? The purpose of this photographic documentary was to provide an inventory of Berggasse 19 so exact that, as Aichhorn envisioned it, the home of psychoanalysis might be painstakingly re-created as a museum after the impending war.[1] Engelman, a mechan-

1. See Edmund Engelman, "A Memoir," which follows the published English-language version of the photographs, *Berggasse 19: Sigmund Freud's Home and Offices, Vienna 1938* (New York: Basic Books, 1976), 134. Rita Ransohoff's photographic captions visually orient the reader, while Peter Gay's preface to the volume, "Freud: For the Marble Tablet," provides an eloquent historical and biographical introduction. See also the more recent German edition of Engelman's photographs, *Sigmund Freud: Wien IX. Berggasse 19* (Vienna: Verlag Christian Brandstätter, 1993), which includes an introduction by Inge Scholz-Strasser, general secretary of the Freud Haus.

ical and electrical engineer who ran a local photography shop on the Karntnerstrasse, agreed to try to provide a pictorial record of Berggasse 19. In the course of four days, using two cameras (a Rolleiflex and a Leica), two lenses (a fifty-millimeter lens and a twenty-eight-millimeter wide-angle lens), and a light meter, and working without the aid of either flashes or floodlights, Engelman took approximately one hundred shots of Berggasse 19, focusing on the consulting room, study, and family living quarters.[2] These photographs,

2. Edmund Engelman, interview by Diana Fuss, September 14, 1995. Of these one hundred photographs, fifty-six have been published in the English-language version of *Berggasse 19*.

together with a short film segment of Freud's office taken by Marie Bonaparte in December 1937, provide the only extant visual record of the place where, for forty-seven years, Freud

treated his patients, met regularly with his colleagues, and wrote his scientific papers and case histories.

Freud's biographers have written eloquently of his traumatic expulsion from his home in Vienna; cultural historians have studied in fascinating detail the peculiarities of Freud's domestic arrangements and the routine of his office schedule; psychoanalysts have analyzed at length the procedures of Freud's clinical practice; and art historians have examined the meaning of Freud's extensive collection of antiquities and the links between psychoanalysis and archaeology. But we have yet to consider the significance of the spatial site that housed these practices and objects. In other words, we have yet to fully enter Berggasse 19. How might the spatial configuration of Freud's office, and the arrangement of furniture and objects within it, frame our understanding of psychoanalytic theory and practice? What might an architectural study of Berggasse 19 tell us about the play of vision, power, and transference that structures the analytic scene?

Taking as a point of departure Engelman's black-and-white photographs, as well as architectural drawings gathered from visits to Freud's offices in London and Vienna, this essay traverses the porous boundary between the two-dimensional space of photography and the three-dimensional space of architecture. The convergence of these two languages of space highlights the confusion of surface and depth, inside and outside, subject and object that characterizes psychoanalysis's own primal scene. Until recently, questions of spectatorship have been theorized largely in terms of a subject's perception of a two-dimensional image (photography, film, television).[3] This study explores the role of

3. An exception is Beatriz Colomina's important analysis of spectatorship in the architectural interiors of Adolf Loos and Le Corbusier in her *Privacy and Publicity: Modern Architecture as Mass Media* (Cambridge: MIT Press, 1994).

both vision and hearing in three-dimensional space, examining how architecture organizes the physical and sensory interaction of bodies as they move through the interior of

Freud's study and consulting room. Architecture and psychoanalysis come together here in a reading of the interior, for both are cultural discourses of the seen and the unseen, of the audible and the inaudible—of public and private space.

This project is impelled by the same powerful fantasy that drives Edmund Engelman's photographs—namely, the illusion that the experience of early psychoanalysis can be relived by retracing the footsteps of Freud's patients. But the space of Freud's office is a fundamentally irrecoverable one. The photographs of Berggasse 19, originally taken for the postwar construction of a Freud museum, have themselves become the museum, miniature sites of preservation and display. Today, visitors to the consulting room and study in Berggasse 19 will find a space emptied of Freud's possessions (currently housed in the Freud Museum in London) but encompassed with enlargements of Engelman's photographs on the walls. This highly unusual mode of museum exhibition insists on the mediating function of the photographs while preserving the empty rooms of the office as a space of exile and absence: the place Freud was finally forced to flee at the end of his life "to die in freedom."[4] To the extent that this

4. Freud to his son Ernst, May 12, 1938, *Sigmund Freud, Briefe 1873–1939*, ed. Ernst L. Freud (Frankfurt: S. Fischer, 1960), 435.

research project is an attempt at recovery, at reconstituting from the fragments of history what has been buried and lost, this reading of Berggasse 19 is inevitably a work of mourning, framed by the same logic of memorialization that so pervasively organized the space of Freud's office.

Engelman's photodocumentary opens with three exterior shots of Berggasse 19, motivated, as he was later to write, by a presentiment that the building itself would be destroyed in the war.[5] The facade of this typical late-

5. Engelman, "Memoir," 136.

nineteenth-century apartment house comes into focus through a sequence of long, medium, and close shots of the entry door. Exerting a kind of centrifugal force, a swastika placed over the door of Berggasse 19 by the building's Aryan owner pulls the camera in, gradually focusing and delimiting the social boundaries of the photodocumentary's visual field. What kind of space is urban street space? For the European, the street is the place of chance encounters and accidental dramas. It is also, historically, the site of political uprising and counterrevolution—the birthplace of the modern revolutionary subject. But as Susan Suleiman notes of the modern wayfare, "After 1933, any attempt to think politically about the street had to grapple with its profound ambiguity."[6] The street, formerly a place of collective

6. Susan Suleiman, "Bataille in the Street: The Search for Virility in the 1930s," *Critical Inquiry* 21 (Autumn 1994): 62.

resistance to state intervention, becomes, with the rise of fascism in Europe, a public venue for Nazi torchlight parades and other forms of national socialist ideology.

Engelman's three views of the street, taken with a wide-angle lens, capture a near-deserted Berggasse. Far from removing us from the sphere of political action, however, these daytime shots of a scarcely populated urban street illuminate, in visually arresting fashion, the realities of political occupation for the predominantly Jewish residents of Vienna's Ninth District. Most of the Ninth District's Jewish population was located on eleven streets, including the Berggasse, which ran from the fashionable upper-middle-class neighborhood of the University of Vienna at one end to the junk shops of the Tandelmarkt, owned by poor Jewish shopkeepers, at the other.[7] Though located just outside the Ringstrasse,

7. Hannah S. Decker, *Freud, Dora, and Vienna, 1900* (New York: Free Press, 1991), 24. Bruno Bettelheim has speculated that Freud's choice of this respectable but undistinguished street was motivated by a deep cultural ambivalence, as Freud sought to reconcile loyalty to his Jewish beginnings with competing desires for assimilationist respectability. See Bettelheim's *Freud's Vienna & Other Essays* (New York: Vintage, 1991), 20. Bettelheim argues in this review of Engelman's photographs that "studying the psychoanalytic couch in detail does not necessarily give any inkling of what psychoanalysis is all about, nor does viewing the settings in which it all happened explain the man, or his work" (19). This reading of Berggasse 19 suggests that just the opposite is the case: Engelman's photographs and the space of the office provide important clues not only to Freud's role as clinician but also to the historical development of psychoanalysis, a practice that evolved in response to the changing social, political, and cultural spaces it inhabited.

the Berggasse was very much at the center of the German occupation. By the time Engelman embarked on his pictorial record of Freud's residence in May 1938, the image of an almost empty urban street operated as a potent sign of political danger and social displacement. For Vienna's Jewish residents, occupation meant incarceration; to be "occupied" was to be exiled, driven out of the public space of the street and into the home.

Operating without the use of a flash, ordinarily employed for interior shots, and continuing to use a wide-angle lens designed for exterior exposures, Engelman transports the codes and conventions of street photography inside Berggasse 19. The building becomes an interior street as the camera's peripatetic gaze traffics through domestic space. Engelman begins his pictorial walking tour by bringing us across the entry threshold and into the lobby, a wide linear space that, with its cobblestone floor and coffered ceiling, resembles a covered arcade. At the end of the entry corridor, a pair of glazed doors, their glass panes etched with antique female figures, provides a view of an aedicule located on axis in the rear service courtyard beyond. These symmetrical, semitransparent doors establish a recurring visual motif that is progressively disrupted and finally displaced as we approach and move through the suite of rooms comprising Freud's office. Interestingly, Berggasse 19 wears its facade on the inside; those architectural elements normally found on the exterior of a building can be seen on the interior of Freud's apartment house. At the top of the switchback stair, for example, we encounter a translucent window, an interior window that looks not onto an exterior courtyard but directly into the Freud family's private apartment. Backlit but draped by an interior curtain, Freud's inside window troubles the traditional distinction between privacy and publicity by rendering completely ambiguous whether we are on the outside looking in or on the inside looking out.

The architectural transposition of public and private space chronicled by Engelman's camera captures Freud's own relationship to his workplace, for although located at the back of the apartment and insulated from the street, Freud's office nonetheless operated as a busy thoroughfare. Patients, colleagues, friends, family, and even pets moved in and out at regular intervals. When he needed privacy, Freud would seek refuge on the Ringstrasse, where he would retreat for his daily constitutional, occasionally with a family member or friend to accompany him. For Freud, the interior space of the office and the exterior space of the street were seamless extensions of one another; both were places of movement and conversation, of chance words and surprise meetings, of accident and incident.[8] The commerce

8. On the street as a site of "accident and incident," see Peter Jukes's introduction to *A Shout in the Street: An Excursion into the Modern City* (Berkeley and Los Angeles: University of California Press, 1990).

of everyday encounters constituted the primary source materials of interior reflection his patients brought to their private sessions with Freud. The transactions of the street quickly became the transferences of the therapeutic scene.

Inside Freud's consulting room and adjoining study, we are confronted with a confusing assortment of furniture and objects: couch, chair, books, bookcases, cabinets, paintings, photographs, lights, rugs, and Freud's extensive collection of antiquities. Freud displayed in the close space of his office the entirety of his collection, acquired mainly from local antique dealers with earnings set aside from his daily hour of open consultations.[9] The experience of viewing

9. Edmund Engelman recollects the experience of visiting Freud's cluttered office as similar to being "inside the storage room of an antique dealer." Engelman, interview.

Engelman's photographs of Freud's office is like nothing so much as window shopping, since we are permitted to view, but not touch, the objects before us, many arranged in glass showcases. Ultimately, what Engelman seeks to document in these photographs is not just the objects but their particular sites of display. It is the very specific spatial arrangement of objects within the interior that constitutes the photodocumentary's visual field and that offers a blueprint for the future reconstruction of the office-museum.

The gaze of Engelman's camera is systematic, not random: it documents and surveys, inventories and catalogs. It moves from one corner of the room to the next, from wall to wall, window to window, memorizing the details of the office interior. This archival gaze is also a slightly manic one, obsessively traversing the same spaces, partitioning the office into a series of overlapping but discrete perceptual fields, at once contiguous and enclosed. The prosthetic eye of the camera attempts to take everything in but finds its efforts frustrated by the very objects it seeks to preserve. The visual space becomes a carceral one as Engelman's camera repeatedly tries, and fails, to negotiate the crowded terrain of Freud's office, so cluttered with objects that many of the two thousand antiquities can be seen in these photographs spilling onto the study floor.[10]

10. As early as 1901, only five years after beginning his collection, Freud writes of the shortage of space in his office study, already filled with pottery and other antiquities, and of his visitors' concerns that he might eventually break something. See Freud's *The Psychopathology of Everyday Life*, vol. 6 of *The Standard Edition of the Complete Psychological Works of Sigmund Freud*, trans. and ed. James Strachey (London: Hogarth Press, 1953–74), 167. Hereafter, all volume and page numbers are cited in the text.

Two months after his father's death in October 1896, Freud began assembling the antiquities that would transform his office into a veritable tomb. The debilitating illness and lingering death of Jakob Freud is generally recognized as the emotional crisis that galvanized Freud's compensatory interest in collecting. A father's demise is "the most important event, the most poignant loss, of a man's life" (4:xxvi), Freud famously opines in *The Interpretation of Dreams*, a book that has itself been read as an extended work of mourning, Freud's gradual coming to terms with the loss of his father. But it is not just his father whom Freud mourns through his accumulation of reliquary objects; it is also, in some profound sense, himself. Freud's self-described "death deliria"[11] played a cen-

11. Freud to Fliess, April 19, 1894, *The Complete Letters of Sigmund Freud to Wilhelm Fliess: 1887–1904*, trans. and ed. Jeffrey Moussaieff Masson (Cambridge: Harvard University Press, 1985), 68.

tral role in shaping the psychical and physical space of his office. Long before his father died, Freud was preoccupied with foretelling the exact time of his own future death. In a letter to Wilhelm Fliess of June 22, 1894, Freud insists that although he has no scientific basis for his predictions, he "shall go on suffering from various complaints for another four to five to eight years, with good and bad periods, and then between forty and fifty perish very abruptly from a rupture of the heart."[12] As Freud moved into the period forecast

12. Freud to Fliess, June 22, 1894, *Complete Letters*, 85.

for his "rupture of the heart," it was not his own death that occurred but that of his father, who fell fatally ill and died of heart failure shortly after Freud's fortieth birthday: "All of it happened in my critical period," Freud writes to Fliess a day after his father's funeral, "and I am really quite down because of it."[13] Freud apparently felt that his father died in his place,

13. Freud to Fliess, October 26, 1896, *Complete Letters*, 201.

prompting a labor of self-entombment that exhausted itself only with Freud's own painful and prolonged death almost half a century later.

Like Osiris buried alive in his coffin,[14] Freud began sur-

14. Freud owned many representations of Osiris, king of the underworld and god of resurrection. Osiris, in some accounts the first Egyptian mummy, was locked into a coffin and set adrift on the Nile. Three different bronze statues of Osiris— two complete figures and a head fragment—adorned Freud's desk, testifying to the importance Freud accorded this particular Egyptian deity.

rounding himself with disinterred objects: Egyptian scarabs, Roman death masks, Etruscan funeral vases, bronze coffins, and mummy portraits.[15] The attempt to chronicle the space

15. For a more complete discussion of Freud's antiquities, see the essays and selected catalog in *Sigmund Freud and Art: His Personal Collection of Antiquities*, ed. Lynn Gamwell and Richard Wells (London: Thames and Hudson, 1989). John Forrester provides an especially fascinating reading of Freud's antiquities in his essay "'Mille e tre': Freud and Collecting," in *The Cultures of Collecting*, ed. John Elsner and Roger Cardinal (Cambridge: Harvard University Press, 1994), 224–51.

of Freud's office for the purposes of erecting a future museum upon its ruins was, by 1938, a touchingly belated act, for Freud's office was a museum long before Engelman arrived to document it. Like all museums, this particular memorial site doubled as a mausoleum, showcasing the self-enshrinement of a collector buried among his funerary objects. "Museum and mausoleum are connected by more than phonetic association," Adorno once commented. "Museums are the family sepulchers of works of art."[16]

16. Theodor Adorno, "Valéry Proust Museum," in *Prisms*, trans. Samuel and Shierry Weber (Cambridge: MIT Press, 1981), 175. Freud's office bears striking similarities to the house-museum of Sir John Soane in London. For a discussion of the museum as a place of entombment, see John Elsner's "A Collector's Model of Desire: The House and Museum of Sir John Soane," in *Cultures of Collecting*, 155–76. See also Douglas Crimp, *On the Museum's Ruins* (Cambridge: MIT Press, 1993).

Engelman's photographs dramatically capture what half a century of Freud commentary has overlooked: the location of the analytic scene within the walls of a crypt. When patients arrived at Freud's office, they entered an overdetermined space of loss and absence, grief and memory, elegy and mourning. In short, they entered the exteriorized theater of Freud's own emotional history, where every object newly found memorialized a love object lost.

We might recall at this juncture that Berggasse 19 was not Freud's first professional office. Freud initially set up his medical practice in a new residential building erected on the ashes of one of Vienna's most famous edifices, the Ring Theater, which burned to the ground in 1881 in a spectacular fire, killing over six hundred people inside. Austria's Franz Josef commissioned the Viennese architect F. V. Schmidt to construct on the ruins an apartment house for the *haute bourgeoisie;* a portion of the rent would be allocated to assist the hundreds of children orphaned by the fire. It was here, in an architectural monument to the dead of Vienna's Ring Theater, that psychoanalysis first took up residence. Not even the birth of the Freuds' first child, which brought the newly married couple an official letter from the emperor congratulating them on

bringing new life to the site of such tragic loss, could completely erase for Freud the symbolic connotations of treating patients' nervous disorders in a place that came to be known as the *Sühnhaus* (House of Atonement).[17] Freud's psychoana-

17. For fuller accounts of the Kaiserliches Stiftungshaus, Freud's first home and office, see Ernest Jones, *The Life and Work of Sigmund Freud* (New York: Basic Books, 1953), 1:149, and Bettelheim, *Freud's Vienna*, 11–12.

lytic practice, from the very beginning, was closely associated with loss and recovery, the work of mourning.

The patient's entry into Freud's office initiates a series of complicated and subtle transactions of power, orchestrated largely by the very precise spatial arrangement of objects and furniture. Freud held initial consultations, between 3:00 and 4:00 every afternoon, in the study section of his office (fig. 1). Preferring a face-to-face encounter with prospective patients, Freud seated them approximately four feet away from himself, across the divide of a table adjacent to his writing desk. Located in the center of a square room, at the intersection of two axial lines, the patient would appear to occupy the spatial locus of power. As if to confirm the illusion of his centrality, the patient is immediately presented, when seated, with a reflection of his own image, in a small portrait-sized mirror framed in gold filigree and hanging, at eye level, on a facing window (fig. 2). As soon as Freud sits down at his desk, however, interposing himself between patient and mirror, the patient's reflection is blocked by Freud's head. Head substitutes for mirror in a metaphorical staging of the clinical role Freud seeks to assume. "The doctor," Freud pronounces in *Papers on Technique*, "should be opaque to his patients and, like a mirror, should show them nothing but what is shown to him" (12:118).

Freud's clinical assumption of the function of the mirror, and the substitution of other for self that it enacts, sets into motion the transferential dynamics that will structure all future doctor-patient encounters. In preparation for the laborious work of overcoming their unconscious resist-

1
Freud's Study
For their first consultation with the doctor, patients were seated in the chair at the very center of the study, surveyed not only by Freud but also by the heads and figurines on the surrounding walls and tables. Many of Freud's 2,500 books lined the walls of the study, also cluttered with antiquities.

2
Study Desk
The patient sees his reflection framed within the portrait-sized mirror on the central mullion of the window behind Freud's desk. When Freud sits in his desk chair, his head blocks and replaces the patient's image in the mirror, initiating the transferential dynamics governing future therapeutic encounters.

ances, patients are required to divest themselves of authority while seated in the very center of power. In a reverse
panopticon, the most central location in Freud's study (the
point from which the gaze normally issues) turns out to be
the most vulnerable, as the patient suddenly finds himself
exposed on all sides to a multitude of gazes. Viewed from
both left and right by a phalanx of ancient figurines (all displayed at eye level and arranged to face the patient), as well
as from behind by a collection of detached antique heads
and from the front by Freud's imposing visage, the patient is
surveyed from every direction. Power in this transferential
scene is exercised from the margins. From the protected
vantage point of his desk chair, Freud studies his patient's
face, fully illuminated by the afternoon light, while his own
face remains barely visible, almost entirely eclipsed by
backlighting from the window behind him.

"The process of psychoanalysis," Freud goes on to remark
in *Papers on Technique*, "is retarded by the dread felt by the
average observer of seeing himself in his own mirror" (12:210).
The analogy of the mirror, used to describe the process of
psychoanalytic self-reflection, makes its first appearance in
Freud's work in his reading of the memoirs of Daniel Paul
Schreber. Mirrors figure prominently in Schreber's transvestic
identification: "Anyone who should happen to see me before the
mirror with the upper portion of my torso bared—especially if
the illusion is assisted by my wearing a little feminine finery—
would receive an unmistakable impression of a *female bust*"
(12:33). And what did Freud see when, alone in his office
among his classical heads and ancient figurines, he turned to
face his own image in the mirror? Freud, too, saw the unmistakable impression of a bust—head and shoulders severed
from the body, torsoless and floating, like the Roman head
overlooking his consulting-room chair or the death mask displayed in his study. His head decapitated by the frame of the
mirror, Freud is visually identified with one of his own classical
sculptures, transformed into a statuary fragment.

Looking in the other direction Freud also saw only
heads. A wooden statue of a Chinese sage sitting on the
table between Freud and his patient severs the patient's
head in the same way Freud's head is decapitated by the
frame of the mirror. From the vantage point of the desk
chair, the patient's disembodied head assumes the status
of one of Freud's antiquities, homologous not only to the
stone heads filling the table directly behind the patient (the
only table in the office displaying almost exclusively heads)
but also to the framed photographic portraits above them,
hanging at the same level as the mirror.

For Freud, every self-reflection reveals a death mask,
every mirror image a spectral double. In his meditation on
the theme of doubling, Freud remarks in "The 'Uncanny'"
that while the double first emerges in our psychical lives as
a "preservation against extinction," this double (in typically
duplicitous fashion) soon reverses itself: "From having been
an assurance of immortality, it becomes the uncanny har-
binger of death" (17:235). By captivating our image, immo-
bilizing and framing it, the mirror reveals a picture of our
own unthinkable mortality.

Yet as Freud notes elsewhere, it is finally impossible to
visualize our own deaths, for "whenever we attempt to do so
we can perceive that we are in fact still present as spectators" (14:289). The mirror that memorializes also reincar-
nates, reconstituting us as phantom spectators, witnesses
to our own irreplaceability. The mirror thus functions simultaneously like a window, assisting us in passing through
the unrepresentable space of our violent eradication and
helping us, in effect, in surviving our own deaths. This was
indeed the function of Etruscan mirrors (so prominent in
Freud's private collection) on whose polished bronze surfaces mythological scenes were engraved. By differentiat-
ing between pictorial space and real space, the frames of
Etruscan mirrors offer the illusion of a view onto another
world. These mirrors, originally buried in tombs, assisted

their owners in passing through their deaths: the Etruscan mirror opened a window onto immortality.

Lacan saw as much in his early reflections on the mirror stage. Radically dislocating the traditional opposition of transparency and reflectivity (window and mirror), Lacan instructs us to "think of the mirror as a pane of glass. You'll see yourself in the glass and you'll see objects beyond it."[18]

18. Jacques Lacan, *Seminar I: Freud's Papers on Technique*, ed. Jacques-Alain Miller, trans. John Forrester (New York: Norton, 1988), 141.

In Freud's office, the placement of a mirror on a window further complicates this conflation of transparency and reflectivity by frustrating the possibility of opening up the space of looking that both crystalline surfaces appear to offer. Normally, when mirrors are placed against opaque walls, they have the capacity to act as windows; they dematerialize and dissolve architectural edges, creating the illusion of extension and expanding the spatial boundaries of the interior. But in this highly peculiar instance of a mirror superimposed on a window, visual access is obstructed rather than facilitated. Unlike the glass panes on Berggasse 19's rear entry doors, which allow the viewer's gaze to pass easily along a central axis from inside to outside, the composition of Freud's study window, with the mirror occupying the central vanishing point, redirects the gaze inward. By forcing the subject of reflection to confront an externalized gaze relayed back upon itself, the mirror on Freud's window interrupts the reassuring classical symmetries of self and other, inside and outside, seeing and being seen.[19]

19. For an excellent discussion of challenges to the traditional humanism of the architectural window, see Thomas Keenan, "Windows: Of Vulnerability," in *The Phantom Public Sphere*, ed. Bruce Robbins (Minneapolis: University of Minnesota Press, 1994), 121–41. See also Colomina, *Privacy and Publicity*, esp. 80–82, 234–38, and 283 ff. An earlier discussion of windows and mirrors can be found in Diana Agrest, "Architecture of Mirror/Mirror of Architecture," in *Architecture from Without: Theoretical Framings for a Critical Practice* (Cambridge: MIT Press, 1991), 139–55.

Instead, the architectonics of the Freudian subject depends fundamentally upon a spatial dislocation, upon seeing the self exteriorized. It is not only that when we look in the mirror we see how others see us but also that we see ourselves occupying a space where we are not. The figure that confronts us in the mirror permits us to look not just at but through ourselves to the "object who knows himself to be seen."[20] The domain delimited by Lacan's *imago,* "the

20. Lacan, *Seminar I*, 215. See also 78.

statue in which man projects himself,"[21] is thus a strangely

21. Jacques Lacan, "The Mirror Stage as Formative of the Function of the I as Revealed in Psychoanalytic Experience," in *Écrits*, trans. Alan Sheridan (New York: Norton, 1977), 2.

lifeless one. As Mikkel Borch-Jacobsen pictures it in "The Statue Man," this mirror world is "a sort of immense museum peopled with immobile 'statues,' 'images' of stone, and hieratic 'forms.'" It is "the most inhuman of possible worlds, the most *unheimlich*."[22]

22. Mikkel Borch-Jacobsen, *Lacan: The Absolute Master*, trans. Douglas Brick (Stanford: Stanford University Press, 1991), 59.

What Freud sees in his mirror is a subject who is, first and foremost, an object, a statue, a bust. The "dread" of self-reflection that Freud describes in *Papers on Technique* appears to issue from a fear of castration, of dramatic bodily disfigurement. If, as Freud insists in "Medusa's Head," the terror of castration is always linked to the sight of something, then it is the sight of *seeing oneself seeing* that possesses lethal consequences for the figure in the mirror. Like Medusa, who is slain by the fatal powers of her own gaze reflected back to her by Perseus's shield, Freud's narcissistic gaze makes him "stiff with terror, turns him to stone" (18:273). Self-reflection petrifies. Perhaps this is the knowledge that so frightened, and so fascinated, Freud: the realization that the subject's "optical erection" could be achieved only at the price of its castration, its instantaneous, fatal transformation into a broken relic.

As the clinical treatment moves from the initial consultation in Freud's study to the sessions on the consulting-room couch, the distribution of objects in the room produces a new kind of body, and a reconfigured doctor-patient relationship (fig. 3). In the study, the patient, sitting isolated and exposed at the center of the room, occupied the point of maximum exposure; in the consulting room, the patient finds herself securely situated outside a circuit of visual surveillance. The arrangement of couch and chair, with their occupants facing outward at perpendicular angles, ensures that, once the analysis formally begins, there will never be an unobstructed line of vision between patient and doctor. The most intimate space in the room is thus also the most highly mediated, as if such close physical proximity between patient and doctor can be sustained only by the structural elimination of any direct visual transaction. The placement of articles on and around the consulting-room couch—the heavy Persian rug hung from the wall and anchored to the couch by a matching rug, the chenille cushions supporting the patient's head, neck, and upper back, and the blanket and porcelain stove warming the patient's feet—creates the impression of a protected enclave, a room within a room, a private interior space.

The profusion of sensuous Oriental rugs and throw pillows, and the horsehair sofa in the consulting room in Berggasse 19, suggests the subtle encroachment of "female" domestic space into the public sphere of the office. Freud's professional office as a scene of domestic comfort is precisely how the Wolf Man remembered it thirty-eight years after the completion of his formal analysis:

> I can remember, as though I saw them today, his
> two adjoining studies, with the door open
> between them and with their windows opening
> on a little courtyard. There was always a feeling
> of sacred peace and quiet here. The rooms
> themselves must have been a surprise to any
> patient, for they in no way reminded one of
> a doctor's office . . . A few potted plants added
> life to the rooms, and the warm carpet and cur-

tains gave them a homelike note. Everything
here contributed to one's feeling of leaving the
haste of modern life behind, of being sheltered
from one's daily cares.[23]

23. *The Wolf Man, by the Wolf Man*, ed. Muriel Gardiner (New York: Noonday, 1991), 139. Sergei Pankeiev (the Wolf Man) also takes note, as all Freud's patients did, of the many objects in the room: "Here were all kinds of statuettes and other unusual objects, which even the layman recognized as archeological finds from ancient Egypt. Here and there on the walls were stone plaques representing various scenes of long-vanished epochs . . . Freud himself explained his love for archaeology in that the psychoanalyst, like the archeologist in his excavations, must uncover layer after layer of the patient's psyche, before coming to the deepest, most valuable treasures" (139). For more on the dominance of the archaeological metaphor in Freud's work, see Donald Kuspit, "A Mighty Metaphor: The Analogy of Archaeology and Psychoanalysis," in Gamwell and Wells, *Sigmund Freud and Art*, 133–51.

In her autobiographical work *Tribute to Freud*, the American poet H.D. recalls Freud's office in similar terms, emphasizing the feelings of safety and security generated by the space encompassing the consulting-room couch: "Today, lying on the famous psychoanalytical couch, . . . [w]herever my fantasies may take me now, I have a center, security, aim. I am centralized or reoriented here in this mysterious lion's den or Aladdin's cave of treasures."[24]

24. H.D., *Tribute to Freud* (New York: McGraw-Hill, 1975), 132. Hereafter, cited in the text with the abbreviation *TF*. H.D.'s account of her psychoanalytic sessions with Freud provides us with the most complete recollection we have, from the point of view of a patient, of Freud's consulting room. Her memoir offers a narrative counterpart to Engelman's photographs, describing, in rich detail, the view from the couch and the sounds, smells, and objects around her.

H.D. goes on to describe the "smoke of burnt incense" (*TF*, 23) and the "fumes of the aromatic cigar" (*TF*, 132) that waft above the couch, emanating from the invisible corner behind her. In fact, Freud considered his passion for collecting "an addiction second in intensity only to his nicotine addiction."[25] The air in Freud's treatment room, densely

25. Max Schur, *Freud: Living and Dying* (New York: International University Press, 1972), 246.

humidified by ceramic water tubes attached to the Viennese stove, hung heavy with the smell of Freud's favorite cigars,

3

Freud's Consulting Room

The arrangement of couch and chair creates a warm, protected, intimate corner for the analytic conversation. The silent sitting figures carved out of stone, depicted in the picture of the temple of Ramses II hanging over the couch, may have struck Freud as classical prototypes for the sedentary analyst, required to listen patiently for long hours.

which he often smoked during analytic sessions. From reading the visual record of Freud's office alongside these verbal accounts, a carefully staged Orientalist scene insistently begins to take shape. Reclining on an ottoman couch, cushioned by Eastern carpets, and wreathed in pungent smoke, patients find themselves at home in a late Victorian fantasy of the opium den.

In Europe's fin-de-siècle fascination with the East, Oriental interiors—especially the smoking room—were closely associated with leisure and relaxation. The bright dyes, luxurious textures, and bold designs of increasingly popular Persian carpets were instrumental in importing into the bourgeois Victorian home a stereotypical aura of Eastern exoticism. In fact, the last decades of the nineteenth century found Europe in the grip of what one German design historian has called "Oriental carpet fever."[26] The first major European

26. Friedrich Spuhler, *Oriental Carpets in the Museum of Islamic Art, Berlin,* trans. Robert Pinner (London: Faber and Faber, 1988), 10. See also David Sylvester, "On Western Attitudes to Eastern Carpets," in *Islamic Carpets from the Joseph V. McMullan Collection* (London: Arts Council of Great Britain, 1972); Kurt Erdmann, *Seven Hundred Years of Oriental Carpets,* ed. Hanna Erdmann, trans. May H. Beattie and Hildegard Herzog (London: Faber and Faber, 1970); and John Mills, "The Coming of the Carpet to the West," in *The Eastern Carpet in the Western World, from the 15th to the 17th Century,* ed. Donald King and David Sylvester (London: Arts Council of Great Britain, 1983). For a more detailed treatment of Orientalism in the context of Western architecture and interior design, see John M. MacKenzie's *Orientalism: History, Theory and the Arts* (Manchester: Manchester University Press, 1995). While many of the older carpets on display in the Vienna exhibition came from mosques, Freud's newer carpets were woven in northwest Persia, most likely in court workshops.

exhibition of Oriental carpets took place at the Imperial Austrian Trade Museum in Vienna in 1891, the very year Freud moved his home and office to Berggasse 19. These Persian carpets and Oriental fabrics may have reminded Freud of his father, by profession a wool merchant who traded in Eastern textiles. For Freud's patients, the enchantment and mystery of these Oriental rugs further sequestered them in the interiorized, reclusive space of the consulting-room couch, a place of private fantasy and quixotic danger, a "mysterious lion's den or Aladdin's cave of treasures."

As if in compensation for the risks that must be taken there, Freud envelops the patient on the couch in all the comforts of a private boudoir, ordinarily the most interior and secluded room of the Viennese home. Freud's office, in fact, is located in the back wing of what was originally designed as part of a domestic residence, in that area of the apartment house typically used as sleeping quarters.[27] It was the sexual

27. Freud's first office in Berggasse 19 was located on the building's ground floor, beneath the family apartment, in three rooms formerly occupied by Victor Adler. Freud conducted his practice here from 1891 to 1907, when he moved his offices into the back rooms of the apartment immediately adjacent to the family residence.

overtones of the famous couch—the sofa as bed—that most discomfited Freud's critics and, if Freud himself is to be believed, no small number of his patients.[28] In one of the

28. Freud admits toward the end of *Papers on Technique* that "a particularly large number of patients object to being asked to lie down, while the doctor sits out of sight behind them" (12:139).

few essays to take note of the spatial organization of the scene of analysis, Luce Irigaray has pointed out that the sexual connotations of lying supine can vary dramatically depending on the sex of the patient. A woman reclining on her back with a man seated erect behind her finds her relation to the doctor inevitably eroticized.[29] The same could be said for

29. Luce Irigaray, "The Gesture in Psychoanalysis," in *Between Feminism and Psychoanalysis,* ed. Teresa Brennan (New York and London: Routledge, 1989), 129.

Freud's male patients, whose daily sessions of private sex talk with their male doctor tacitly homoeroticized the clinical encounter. "Some men," Freud once commented, "scatter small change out of their trouser pockets while they are lying down during treatment and in that way pay whatever fee they think appropriate for the session" (6:214). The association of lying down with scattered change—in short, of sex with money—invokes the specter of (male) prostitution, a connection that Freud appears to intuit here but not fully register.

What is being staged, or restaged, around the privileged, centralized, overinvested figure of the consulting-room couch? "I cannot put up with being stared at by other people for eight hours a day (or more)," Freud acknowledges, defending his mandate that all patients, without exception, assume a reclining position on the couch. But why a couch? The couch is yet another museum relic—a "remnant," Freud calls it, "of the hypnotic method out of which psycho-analysis was evolved" (12:133). While Freud abandoned his early practice of placing patients into a somnambulistic sleep, he retained the couch as a serviceable memorial to psycho-analysis in its infancy. The couch, given to Freud as a gift by his former patient Madame Benveniste around 1890, operated as a nostalgic reminder of his professional past.

But there is more to this couch than its store of personal memories for the doctor; the analytic couch served a mnemonic function for the patient as well. An anecdote recounted by Freud in *The Psychopathology of Everyday Life* provocatively suggests a different way of thinking about the prominence of the consulting-room couch: "A young lady suddenly flung open the door of the consulting room though the woman who preceded her had not yet left it. In apologizing she blamed her 'thoughtlessness'; it soon turned out that she had been demonstrating the curiosity that in the past had caused her to make her way into her parent's bedroom" (6:214).

What is being subtly replayed here, across the threshold of two rooms, is none other than the spectacle of the primal scene. The patient in the waiting room, hearing sounds through the consulting-room door, bursts into Freud's office, propelled by the same "curiosity" that drew her, as a child, to cross the threshold of her parents' private bedchamber. Freud's intruding female hysteric sees all too clearly the highly eroticized choreography made possible by the very particular configuration of consulting-room couch and chair, so closely juxtaposed that if the arm of the couch and the arm of the chair behind it were removed, the patient's head (formerly propped at a thirty-five-degree angle) would fall nearly into Freud's lap. Shortly after this incident of analysis *interruptus,* Freud soundproofed his consulting room by adding a second set of doors lined with red baize. The sound barrier between treatment room and waiting room now insulated the analytic couple, whose muffled voices previously risked transporting the patient in the next room back to the trauma of the primal scene, to that interior place of fantasy where "uncanny sounds" are registered but only belatedly understood.

Freud's own placement in this scene is by no means a simple one; the question of the analyst's identificatory position is far more complicated than Irigaray's "orthogonal"[30]

30. Irigaray, "Gesture in Psychoanalysis," 128.

pair of prone patient/erect doctor might suggest. Significantly, Freud chooses to assume a passive position in his exchange with the patient. Advising against the taking of notes during treatment sessions, a practice that would prohibit the doctor from maintaining a posture of "evenly suspended attention" (12:111), Freud recommends that the analyst "should simply listen, and not bother about whether he is keeping anything in mind." This passive listening technique represents the exact correlative to the fundamental rule of analysis for patients, the injunction to say anything that enters one's head "without selection or censorship" (12:112).[31] The ana-

31. Freud's own practice was to take notes from memory after all his sessions that day had been completed. For particularly important dream texts, the patient was asked to repeat the dream until Freud had committed its details to memory (12:113–14).

lyst must never engage in the work of scientific research while involved in the clinical act of listening. He must instead make himself vulnerable and receptive; he must "lay . . . [himself] open to another person" (12:116); he must allow himself "to be taken by surprise" (12:114).

To put it in a formula: the analyst must turn his own unconscious like a receptive organ toward the transmitting unconscious of the patient. He must adjust himself to the patient as a telephone receiver is adjusted to the transmitting microphone. Just as the receiver converts back into sound waves the electric oscillations in the telephone line that were set up by sound waves, so the doctor's unconscious is able, from the derivatives of the unconscious that are communicated to him, to reconstruct that unconscious that has determined the patient's free associations (12:115–16).

Opening himself to the risk of feminization, Freud assumes the role of an orifice, a listening ear, while the patient becomes a mouth, an oral transmitter. The only telephone in Freud's office was the circuit of communication between analyst and analysand; Freud, as office receptionist, opens a direct line to the patient, adjusting the patient's unconscious to the frequencies of his own psychical interior. This interconnection between patient and doctor, transmitter and receiver, mouth and ear sets up a technology of oral transmission: transference operates telephonically.[32]

32. It is difficult to imagine Freud as a listening ear, the completely passive receptacle of his patients' uncensored speech. Freud's own case histories—from *Dora* (7:1–122) to "The Psychogenesis of a Case of Homosexuality in a Woman" (18:145–72)—reveal that, in the therapeutic encounter, he communicated in a more interactive way than the metaphor of doctor as telephone receiver would imply, often challenging and redirecting patients' ostensibly "free" associations.

After his surgery for oral cancer in 1923, Freud lost much of the hearing in his right ear. His biographer Peter Gay writes that Freud actually moved the couch from one wall to another so he could listen better with his left ear.[33]

33. Peter Gay, *Freud: A Life for Our Time* (New York: Anchor Books, 1988), 427.

The gratification Freud's listening ear derived from the "electric oscillations" of the transferential line suggests that at the center of psychoanalysis's primal scene is a performance of what Neil Hertz has dubbed "oral intercourse in that other sense of the term." Freud's choice of a telephone to describe the intimate exchanges between doctor and patient highlights the "epistemological promiscuity" that characterizes psychoanalysis's therapeutic practice.[34] The

34. Neil Hertz, "Dora's Secrets, Freud's Techniques," in *In Dora's Case: Freud, Hysteria, Feminism*, ed. Charles Bernheimer and Claire Kahane (New York: Columbia University Press, 1985), 229, 234.

very arrangement of couch and chair facilitates an erotics of

voice, privileging sound over sight, speech over spectatorship. In the consulting room, telephone replaces mirror as the governing topos of the doctor-patient relationship.

However, like the mirror on the window, Freud's imaginary telephone immediately connects us to the place of mourning. This indeed is the lesson of Avital Ronell's *The Telephone Book*, which reminds us that the telephone has always been involved in a hermeneutics of mourning, in a call to an absent other: "Like transference, the telephone is given to us as effigy."[35] Invented originally as a device for the

35. Avital Ronell, *The Telephone Book: Technology, Schizophrenia, Electric Speech* (Lincoln: University of Nebraska Press, 1989), 84. See also 88–96.

hearing and speech impaired, the telephone works as a prosthesis to compensate for radical loss. Freud's ear detected in the electric speech of the telephone the soft reverberations of distant connections, the sound of the unconscious. A powerful transmitter of disembodied presence, Freud's telephone was capable of summoning the very spirits of the dead, modulated voices from beyond the grave.

In one respect, the arrangement of bodies in the consulting room bears a certain disquieting resemblance to a wake, with Freud holding vigil over the body of his patient lying immobilized on the couch, most likely enshrouded (mummylike) in the blanket provided, and surrounded by hundreds of funerary objects. *Eros* and *thanatos* turn out to be comfortable bedfellows as Freud's analytic couch doubles as not just bed but bier. Occupying the space of an off-screen presence, the analyst's listening ear and ventriloquized speech offer the patient the promise of reestablishing a tenuous connection to the other who has been lost. By assuming the position of telephone receiver, the one who accepts the call to the other, Freud thus finds himself addressing the patient from the borderline between presence and absence— the threshold between life and death.

In the minds of his patients, Freud was not only healer, prophet, and shaman but gatekeeper to the underworld, "patron of gate-ways and portals" [*TF*, 106]. Like the stone Janus head on his office desk, Freud "faced two ways, as doors and gates opened and shut" [*TF*, 100].[36] A modern-day

36. Psychoanalysis generally reads the space of the doorway in Proustian fashion, as a symbol of change and transition, but in at least one instance the doorway became for Freud a powerful image of arrested movement. In a letter to Minna Bernays of May 20, 1938, written as he anxiously awaited permission to emigrate, Freud compares the experience of impending exile to "standing in the doorway like someone who wants to leave a room but finds that his coat is jammed." *The Diary of Sigmund Freud, 1929–1939,* trans. Michael Molnar [New York: Charles Scribner's Sons, 1992], 236.

Hermes or Thoth, Freud kept vigilant watch over the dangerous passage across the invisible borders of past and present, memory and forgetting. "In analysis," Freud once explained to H.D., "the person is dead after the analysis is over," to which H.D. responded, "Which person?" [*TF*, 141]. With characteristic acuity, H.D. complicates the notion of physician as mourner, alluding to the possibility that it is Freud himself who is mourned, Freud who may already find himself on the other side of the portal. In the journey through death staged by the work of analysis, the question of who is the traveler and who the guide remains, at the very least, open.

In one of Freud's most interesting metaphorizations of the scene of treatment, he imagines doctor and patient as fellow passengers on a railway journey. Tutoring the patient on the technique of free association, Freud recommends: "Act as though . . . you were a traveler sitting next to the window of a railway carriage and describing to someone inside the carriage the changing views which you see outside" [12:135]. The train, associated throughout Freud's work with death and departure, carries doctor and patient along the same track, advancing the familiar genre of the travelogue as a model for the talking cure. The picture of easy companionship and leisurely conversation that Freud paints for his patient clearly seeks to domesticate what threatens to be a terrifying venture. Yet what is particularly striking about Freud's scenario of the fellow train travelers is his own severely circumscribed role within it, for Freud is the passenger whose vision is impaired, who can only imagine the view outside the window that his companion is invited to describe. While doctor and patient are located on the same side of the window, the patient alone is visually empowered while Freud is functionally blinded. Freud can listen but he cannot see; hearing must compensate for a radical loss of vision. Once again, then, Freud imagines himself as a passive, responsive organ: "two open ears and one temporal lobe lubricated for reception."[37]

37. Freud to Fliess, June 30, 1896, *Complete Letters*, 193.

In depriving himself of visual authority, Freud assumes the role of the blind seer, the one who "sacrifices sight . . . with an eye to seeing at last."[38] Through his figurative self-blind-

38. Jacques Derrida, *Memoirs of the Blind: The Self-Portrait and Other Ruins*, trans. Pascale-Anne Brault and Michael Naas [Chicago and London: University of Chicago Press, 1993], 30. In this elegant book, Derrida traces a tradition of prints and drawings depicting figures of blindness, including three of the visionary blind men alluded to here: Oedipus, Tiresias, and Tobit.

ing, Freud inserts himself into a long line of blind healers and sightless soothsayers: Oedipus, the guilty son, who achieves wisdom by putting out his own eyes; Tiresias, the prophet of two sexes, who suffers blindness at the hands of the goddess Hera after testifying to women's greater sexual pleasure; and Tobit, the man of last respects, who never stops asking his sons to close his eyes as the time approaches for his own burial. It is impossible to forget the dream Freud had on the night after his own father's funeral, a dream about closing the eyes. Freud dreamed that he was in a place [in one account, a railway station] where a sign was posted that read "You are requested to close the eyes." Late for his own father's funeral, Freud reads this dream as an expression of guilt for his failure to give his father a proper burial. Freud explains that "The sentence on the sign has a double meaning: one should do one's duty to the dead [an apology as though I had not done it and were in need of leniency], and the actual duty itself. The dream thus stems from the inclination to self-reproach that regularly sets in among survivors."[39]

39. Freud recounts this dream both in his letter to Fliess of November 2, 1896 [*Complete Letters*, 202] and later, in slightly altered form, in *The Interpretation of Dreams* [4:317–18]. See also Freud's analysis of another deathbed dream, "Father on his death-bed like Garibaldi" [5:427–29].

"You are requested to close the eyes" refers to the literal act of performing a burial rite and to the symbolic necessity of taking leave of the dead. As Didier Anzieu perceptively notes, however, the request to "close the eyes" is also one of the instructions Freud habitually gave to his patients when beginning an analytic session.[40] The clinical

40. Didier Anzieu, *Freud's Self-Analysis*, trans. Peter Graham (Madison, Conn.: International University Press, 1986), 172.

rehearsal of this particular ritual provides what is perhaps the clearest illustration of the extent to which Freud envisioned the work of psychoanalysis as an elaborate funeral rite. Freud eventually discontinued the practice of enjoining his patients to close their eyes,[41] but vision and blindness

41. Freud discontinued the practice in 1904. See Anzieu, *Freud's Self-Analysis*, 64.

continued to define for Freud the core dynamic of the therapeutic relationship. Eyes now open, the patient on Freud's consulting-room couch encounters the penetrating look of Wilhelm Jensen's Gradiva, a plaster bas-relief hanging on the wall at the foot of the ottoman, carefully positioned to stare directly down at the patient. It is Gradiva—for Freud the very incarnation of immortality—who offers patient and doctor (eye and ear) a new set of instructions: "Look, but not with bodily eyes, and listen, but not with physical ears. And then . . . the dead wakened" (9:16).

In Freud's theater of inversions, where a healing ritual can lull the living into a netherworld of dreams and a funeral rite can waken the dead, subjects and objects are also transposed. When H.D. first enters the office in Berggasse 19, it is the objects, not their owner, that seize her attention: "The statues stare and stare and seem to say, what has happened to you?" (*TF*, 110). There are more sculptures in Freud's vast collection of antiquities than any other kind of art object, figures with a more immediate and anthropomorphic presence than either painting or photography.[42]

42. Lynn Gamwell has noted that "Almost every object Freud acquired is a figure whose gaze creates a conscious presence." See her "The Origins of Freud's Antiquities Collection," in Gamwell and Wells, *Sigmund Freud and Art*, 27.

Apparently these statues are endowed with the vision that Freud himself is denied; the figurines, their faces and their sight animated, stand in obverse relation to Freud, his face composed and his eyes veiled. In one of H.D.'s only physical descriptions of Freud, she describes him as though she were appreciating a piece of statuary sculpted by an expert craftsman: "His beautiful mouth seemed always slightly smiling, though his eyes, set deep and slightly asymmetrical under the domed forehead (with those furrows cut by a master chisel) were unrevealing. His eyes did not speak to me" (*TF*, 73).

The portals of Freud's eyes were closed to his patients, as if he himself were an inanimate statue. By prohibiting the patient from looking at him during analysis, Freud, ostensibly seeking to ward off the possibility of idolatry, actually lays its foundations. Positioning himself in the place of the "one who must not be looked at," Freud immediately assumes the status of an otherworldly presence concealed behind the inscrutable exterior of a powerful and mysterious graven image.

Is this why the view from Freud's consulting-room chair resists all attempts to reproduce it technologically? And why Engelman's camera, when it attempts to see the space of the office through Freud's eyes, is effectively rendered blind? "I wanted to see things the way Freud saw them, with his own eyes, during the long hours of his treatment sessions and as he sat writing," Engelman concedes in his memoir, "[but] I couldn't . . . fit my bulky tripod into the tight space between Freud's chair at the head of the couch and the little table covered with an oriental rug on which [were] set a half-dozen fragile looking Egyptian statuettes."[43] Unable to simulate the view from the analyst's

43. Engelman, "Memoir," 137.

chair, Engelman finds that he must redirect his gaze back to the perspective of the patient. The consulting-room chair stands as a fundamentally uninhabitable space, a tribute to the imposing figure of the analyst who remains, even to the searching eye of the camera, totally and enigmatically other.

"Tucked" away in his "three-sided niche" (TF, 22), Freud once again can be seen to occupy a spatially marginalized position. But while Freud's physical mobility in the consulting room was more severely restricted than that of his patient, his field of vision was actually far greater. From his treatment chair, Freud could see not only the cabinet of antiquities below the now famous reproduction of Pierre Albert-Brouillet's engraving *La Leçon clinique du Dr. Charcot* but also the room's two main apertures (window and door), which frame it on either side. While from this position he was capable of monitoring any movements in or out of the consulting room, Freud's view of the entry door was partially obscured by a set of fully intact antiquities displayed on the table in front of him, a double row of figurines that, like the patient on the couch, are carefully arranged on a Persian rug. Are we to see these unbroken antiquities as visual surrogates for Freud's patients ("there are priceless broken fragments that are meaningless until we find the other broken bits to match them," H.D. writes [TF, 35]; "I was here because I must not be broken" [TF, 16])?[44] Or are we to

44. H.D. immediately understood the significance of Freud's reliquary objects, their mirror relation to the patients who came to Freud every day to be "skillfully pieced together like the exquisite Greek tear-jars and iridescent glass bowls and vases that gleamed in the dusk from the cabinet" (TF, 14).

see Freud's patients as simply another part of his collection, a conjecture reinforced by the photographs of Marie Bonaparte and Lou-Andreas Salomé, two of Freud's former patients, placed on the study bookcases alongside Freud's other antiquities?

It seems likely that the relationship between Freud's antiquities and his patients was more complex than either of these two possibilities allows. Notably, the Egyptian statues in front of the consulting-room chair were visible to Freud from the side, like the figures in profile found on the

Egyptian papyrus hanging on the wall closest to Freud's immediate line of vision. This particular mummy covering, which depicts a scene of embalming,[45] holds a privileged

45. C. Nicholas Reeves identifies this particular piece of ancient cartonnage as a frontal leg covering from the mummy of a woman. This ancient cartonnage, situated at eye level immediately to the left of the consulting-room chair, offered Freud ample opportunity to reflect on the meaning of death and resurrection, emblematized by the two lower panels, which once again depict Osiris, king of the underworld. For a fuller description of this Egyptian mummy covering and its hieroglyphics, see Gamwell and Wells, *Sigmund Freud and Art*, 75.

place among Freud's antiquities, its location next to the treatment chair permitting hours of careful study. For Freud, interpreting a patient's dream was like deciphering an Egyptian hieroglyph. Pictographic script emblematizes the work of dream interpretation, offering a visual analogue to the template of the dream text, the "picture-language" (13:177) of the unconscious.

From his consulting-room chair, Freud also had an unobstructed view of the desk in the adjoining study, where he adjourned late in the day to take notes on his sessions and to write up his research. "One of the claims of psychoanalysis to distinction is, no doubt, that in its execution research and treatment coincide" (12:114), Freud remarks, immediately qualifying that it is, in fact, unwise to begin scientific research on a case while treatment is still in progress. The architectural design of the office accordingly splits the interior in two, artificially divorcing the space of listening from the space of reflection. But the strict methodological barrier Freud erects between study and consulting room is nonetheless breached by the two doors between them that remain, like listening ears, perpetually open. A single axial line links desk chair to treatment chair, reflection to reception. While Freud listens to the patient from his consulting-room chair, he has a clear view of the desk that awaits him, and a vision of the work of analysis toward which the clinical session aspires. Similarly, while Freud composes his scientific notes and theoretical papers at the study desk, consulting-room couch and chair stand before him like an empty stage set, a visual reminder of the drama that has recently unfolded there, in which Freud himself played a prominent role. The centers of knowledge in these adjoining rooms are thus visually continuous: treatment anticipates research; research rehearses treatment.

The immediate view from Freud's desk chair is no less phantasmatically staged, with many of Freud's favorite figurines lined up in a row on his desktop like so many members of a "silent audience."[46] Freud's desk, the most interior

46. Gamwell, in "Origins of Freud's Antiquities Collection," 28.

place in the office and the most difficult to access, is also the site of greatest structural fortification. Surrounded on three sides by wooden tables, Freud's work area marks out yet another protected enclave, more confining yet more secure than the interior room created for the patient on the couch. It is at his desk that Freud makes the perilous transition from listening to writing; it is at his desk that he enters into dialogue with his professional demons; it is at his desk that he struggles to put his own manuscripts to rest. Visible in Engelman's photographs of the study desk are the spectral outlines of Freud's *Moses and Monotheism,* Freud's last completed work, which, he confesses, "tormented me like an unlaid ghost" [23:103].

In what sense might Freud's office, and the clinical encounter that takes place there, be read not just as an elegiac space but as a haunted one? Freud, it appears, was forever exorcising ghosts. A year after moving his office into a wing of his living quarters, Freud writes to Carl Jung of what he calls his "poltergeist," a cracking noise issuing from the two Egyptian steles resting on top of the oak bookcases. Believing at first that these ancient grave markers are possessed by spirits whenever Jung is in the room, Freud only reluctantly relinquishes his fanciful superstition when the steles continue to groan in his friend's absence: "I confront the despiritualized furniture," Freud laments, "as the poet confronted undeified

Nature after the gods of Greece had passed away."[47]

47. Freud to Jung, April 16, 1909, in *The Freud/Jung Letters*, ed. William McGuire, trans. Ralph Manheim and R. F. C. Hull (Cambridge: Harvard University Press, 1988), 218. This story of the haunted steles appears in the same letter in which Freud analyzes another episode of his death deliria (the superstition that he will die between the ages of sixty-one and sixty-two) and in which he makes reference to what he identifies as "the specifically Jewish nature of my mysticism" (220).

But the Greek gods are not the only apparitions haunting the furniture and antiquities in Freud's office; for Freud's patients, these possessions operate as spectral doubles for the analyst himself. At least once in every analysis, Freud explains, the patient claims that his free associations have stopped; however, if pressed, he will admit that he is thinking of the objects around him—the wallpaper, the gas lamp, the sofa: "Then one knows at once that he has gone off into the transference and that he is engaged upon what are still unconscious thoughts relating to the physician" [18:126].[48]

48. On the subject of a patient's transference onto the doctor through the medium of objects, see also Freud's *Papers on Technique*: "[The patient] had been occupied with the picture of the room in which he was, or he could not help thinking of the objects in the consulting room and of the fact that he was lying here on a sofa . . . [E]verything connected with the present situation represents a transference to the doctor, which proves suitable to serve as a first resistance" [12:138].

A transferential force emanates from Freud's possessions; these overinvested forms operate, for the patient, as shadowy substitutes for the analyst who must not be seen. Whether or not Freud's patients actually related to their physician's objects in this way is perhaps less interesting than the revelation of Freud's own deeply cathected relationship to his things, which his theory of animation implicitly betrays. For this quasi-mystical account of the patient's transference onto the doctor through the medium of surrogate objects is based on Freud's ready presumption that these inanimate possessions *could* somehow function as versions of himself.

The possibility that Freud may identify with these objects, may actually see himself as a part of the vast collection amassed around him, finds ironic visual confirmation in the last of Engelman's office photographs. In the only photograph that includes a human figure, Freud's upper torso and head appear behind the study desk like yet another classical sculpture. Captured in a moment of statuary repose, Freud's imperturbable facial features appear to imitate the bust of him sculpted seven years before by the Yugoslavian artist Oscar Némon. This final image of Freud amid his collection provides eloquent testimony to Jean Baudrillard's claim that, while "a given collection is made up of a succession of terms, . . . the final term must always be the person of the collector," for in the end "it is invariably *oneself* that one collects."[49]

49. Jean Baudrillard, "The System of Collecting," in Eisner and Cardinal, *Cultures of Collecting,* 12.

The very medium of the photograph participates in the process of memorialization that so deeply permeates the space of Freud's office. Theorists of photography inevitably return to the camera's technological capacity to objectify the subject, to turn the image of the living into a memorial to the dead. "The home of the photographed is in fact the cemetery," Eduardo Cadava writes. "A small funerary monument, the photograph is a grave for the living dead."[50] Engelman's

50. Eduardo Cadava, "Words of Light: Theses on the Photography of History," in *Fugitive Images: From Photography to Video*, ed. Patrice Petro (Bloomington and Indianapolis: Indiana University Press, 1995), 223, 224.

camera captures that moment, identified by Roland Barthes, when the one who is photographed is neither subject nor object but a subject becoming an object, a subject who is truly becoming a specter.[51] The photograph of Freud among

51. Roland Barthes, *Camera Lucida: Reflections on Photography*, trans. Richard Howard (New York: Farrar, Straus and Giroux, 1981), 14.

his relics mortifies its living subject; it embalms Freud in a tomb he spent over forty years preparing. It is a suitable memorial to the man who seemed to glimpse, more assuredly than anyone, the many elusive ways in which our deaths anticipate us and our lives encrypt us.

Photography might be said to haunt psychoanalysis in another way, for a principle of photographic likenesses, of double exposures and exposed doubles, animates and reanimates the transferential scene. Insofar as the mechanism of transference works precisely by means of a double exposure—a superimposition of one figure onto another—the process of psychoanalysis can be seen to operate as a form of photographic development. Like photography, the technology of transference performs a kind of spirit work in which the phantoms of missing or lost others come back to life in the person of the analyst. In "Introjection and Transference," Sándor Ferenczi refers to the physician as a "revenant" in whom the patient finds again "the vanished figures of childhood."[52] Freud, as object of his patients' transferences, was

52. Sándor Ferenczi, "Introjection and Transference," *Sex in Psychoanalysis* (New York: Basic Books, 1950), 41.

just such a revenant, the living image of an absent person. Psychoanalysis, in this respect, was never very far from the schools of nineteenth-century spiritualism it so vigorously sought to bury. The ghost of the spirit medium speaks through the psychoanalyst every time the patient, through the agency of transference, communes with the dead.

A year and four months after Engelman took his clandestine photographs of Freud's Vienna office, Freud died of cancer in his new home at 20 Maresfield Gardens in London. He died in his office, a room that had been renovated by his architect son Ernst and arranged by his maid, Paula Fichtl, to reproduce, as closely as possible, the office at Berggasse 19. In this, the most painful period of his sixteen-year battle with oral cancer, Freud's office became his sickroom. It was here that Freud slipped into a coma after Max Schur, at Freud's request, administered the fatal doses of morphine that would end Freud's life on September 23, 1939. Cremated three days later, Freud's ashes were placed, according to the family's wishes, in a Greek urn, a red-figured bell krater presented to Freud as a gift by Marie Bonaparte. Freud at last found a resting place among his beloved antiquities.

ADAPTED FROM *STUD: ARCHITECTURES OF MASCULINITY*, ED. JOEL SANDERS (NEW YORK: PRINCETON ARCHITECTURAL PRESS, 1996).

HOUSE FOR A BACHELOR MINNEAPOLIS, MINNESOTA, 1997–1999

If the design of the traditional suburban house presupposes its inhabitants to be a nuclear family, this project instead reconfigures such a house according to the lifestyle of the contemporary bachelor. Located in a suburban neighborhood just minutes from downtown Minneapolis and built on the foundations of a 1950s Rambler, our design reconfigures the interior in response to our single male client's competing desires for transparency to the outdoors and privacy from neighbors.

The cellular rooms that once characterized the house give way to a sequence of overlapping spaces for work and leisure, zones protected from the prying eyes of neighbors where the bachelor can exercise his mind and body . At the rear property line, an Astroturf fence elevates the level of the horizon, blocking out views of neighboring houses, and then descends and folds horizontally to define a soft ground covering for the subterranean backyard that flows into the master bedroom, creating an indoor-outdoor naturalistic zone where the bachelor can sleep, work out, or lounge by the pool. Architectural finishes (wood paneling, glass, and Astroturf) act like the clothing the bachelor puts on in his dressing room each morning: both applied surfaces enable him to fabricate his identity in the same manner that he constructs his domestic surroundings.

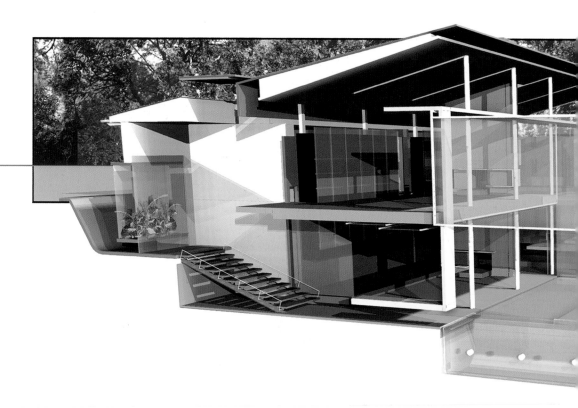

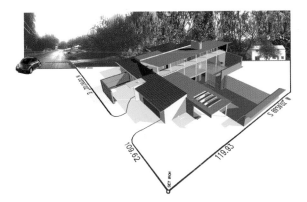

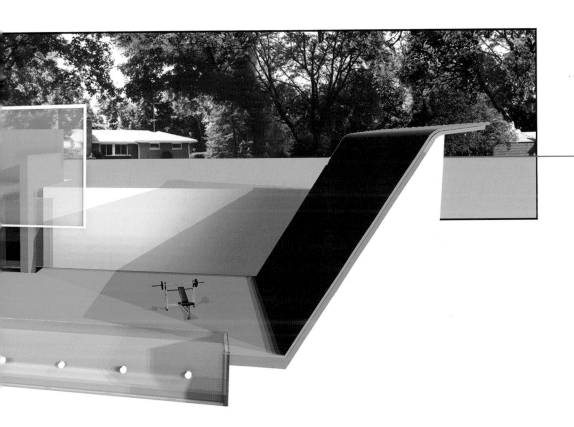

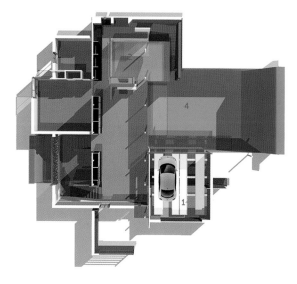

1

Carport

As he parks his car, the bachelor observes his entire domestic domain, framed through the windshield and the rear plate-glass facade of the garage.

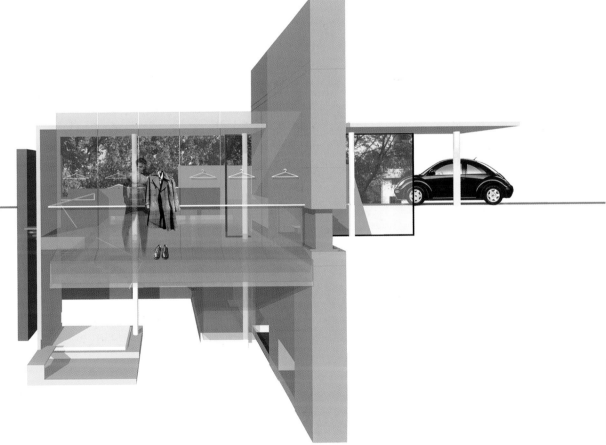

2

Closet

Well aware that clothes make the man, the well-groomed bachelor chooses his daily attire by arranging shirts, jackets, pants, and shoes on aluminum pegs affixed to the rear window wall. Made of semitransparent reflective panels, this garden facade also functions as a mirror, enabling the bachelor to observe the manicured backyard and his own image as he dresses.

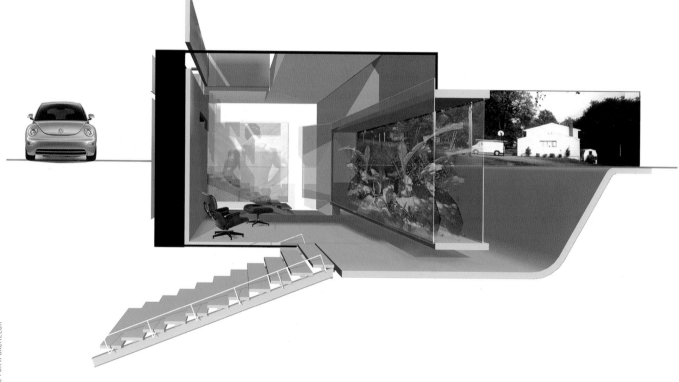

3

Den

In the den, which also doubles as a home office, a tropical-plant-filled terrarium replaces the former picture window, veiling the barren winter landscape outside with a lush image of perpetual summer. The inner surface of this glass vitrine folds to form a projection television screen.

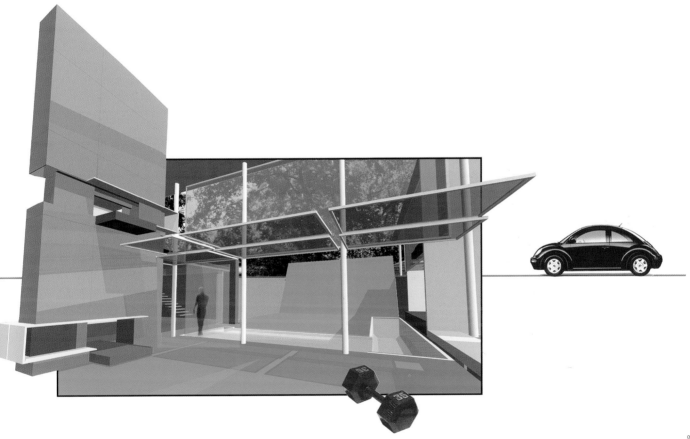

4

Spa

Although located underground, the bedroom spa brings the outside in. Its Astroturf floor provides a resilient surface for lounging or working out beside the lap pool. Likewise, a glass-bottomed pool on the first floor transmits light to the master bedroom below. A curtain of water spills from this aqueous skylight, concealing the silhouettes of showering bodies.

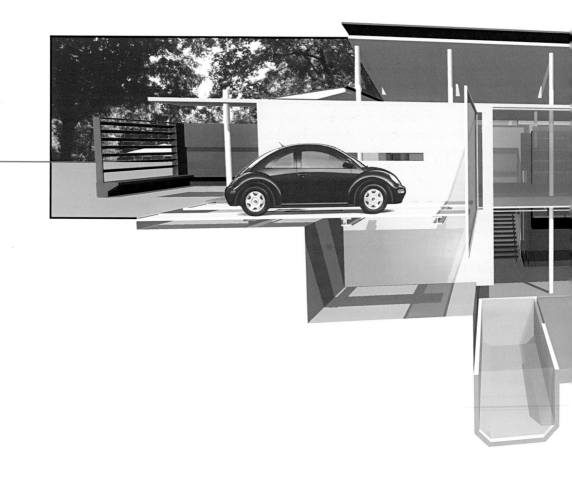

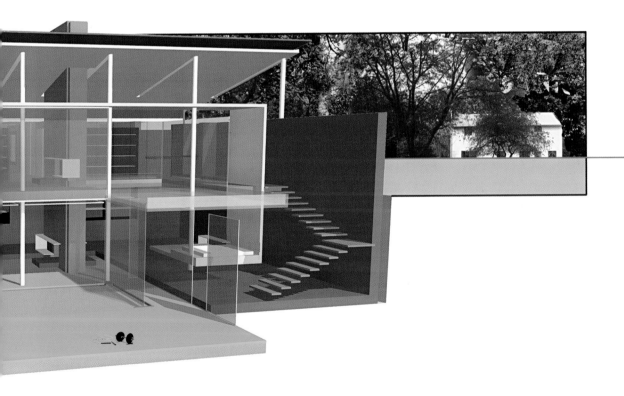

LEE LOFT NEW YORK, NEW YORK, 1997–1999

The Lee loft, a duplex residence in downtown Manhattan, blurs traditional distinctions between architecture, furniture, and fashion, "dressing" the interior in an ensemble of materials that connote masculinity. The master bedroom features inlaid floor tiles, cabinetry veneer, and a bedspread all made of leather. Furniture upholstered in menswear fabrics (gray flannel and suede) complements the extensive surfaces clad in mahogany, a material traditionally associated with boardrooms and men's clubs.

While our design self-consciously deploys materials in order to articulate a single identity—maleness—the Lee loft is also concerned with permitting multiple domestic identities. Consequently, architectural elements possess various uses. Upstairs, the master bedroom doubles as a conversation pit. Mahogany stair treads fold vertically to create a louvered privacy screen and extend horizontally to form bookshelves. Downstairs, on the main living level, sliding glass partitions convert the den into a guest room. The kitchen island is treated as another dual-purpose element: it features a rotating work surface that functions as counter, dining table, or desk.

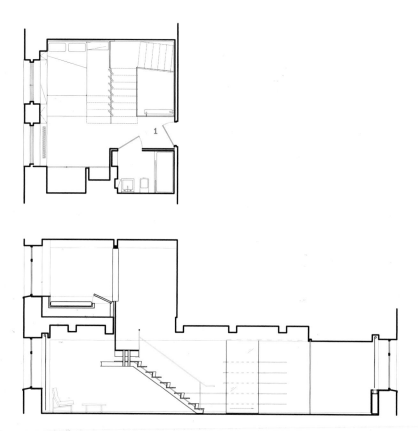

1
Entry
A louvered screen admits natural light to the entry at the same time that it allows the master bedroom to spatially communicate with the rest of the loft.
Hinged floor panels at the perimeter of the platform bed conceal storage compartments and a television that rises by remote control.

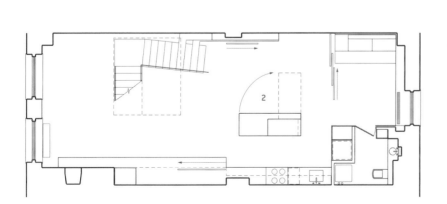

2

Pivoting Kitchen Island
The work surface rotates forty-five degrees to function as a kitchen counter or a dining table.

CURTAIN WARS: ARCHITECTS, DECORATORS, AND THE TWENTIETH-CENTURY DOMESTIC INTERIOR

Curtains, that element of the domestic interior on which the hands of the decorator and the hands of the architect come directly into contact, embody many of the tensions and prejudices that have divided interior designers and architects since the emergence of the professional decorator in the late nineteenth century.[1] Here

1. The term *decorator,* which originally designated an individual who practiced what we today call interior design, is now considered both obsolete and pejorative: it evokes the image of "decoration," a culturally denigrated concept that I will call into question. In the same spirit in which the gay community has revived the once-reviled term *queer,* I will use the labels *decorator* and interior *designer* interchangeably, to both politicize and historicize the activity of "decorating" domestic space.

the hard walls designed by the architect meet the soft fabric that is the decorator's trademark in a juxtaposition that confirms the common perception that architects work conceptually, using durable materials to shape space, while decorators work intuitively, adorning rooms with ephemeral materials and movable objects. Window treatments underscore the divergent design approaches employed by architects and decorators. Architects typically repudiate curtains, believing that this element that modulates vision compromises the architect's conception, obscuring and softening the precise geometry of architectural forms.[2]

2. Frank Lloyd Wright never used curtains and thought of them as "unhygienic." Charles Gwathmey is quoted in the October 2001 *Architectural Digest*: "Interior design 'is a reductive process,' he asserts. 'Decorators think of coming in and adding to "enrich," and I think of our work as the opposite. The interior does not want to be covered up; it does not want to be added to . . . If I design a window wall, the details of that window wall—its materiality, its proportion, the fenestration, the way we control the light—are all integrated and thought about. The idea of coming in and saying, "Let's put a curtain over that!" is totally antipathetical and totally contradictory' " (100).

Decorators, for their part, consider curtains essential; veiling sunlight and views, curtains make domestic privacy possible and offer relief from the austere spaces created by architects often obsessed with form at the expense of comfort. Ironically, the curtain wall, the iconic modernist glass facade that has come to embody so many key values of modern architecture—logic, structural integrity, and stripped-down form—takes its name from the curtain, the signature element of the interior decorator. But are architecture and interior decoration really oppositional practices, or are they, as the term "curtain wall" suggests, more interdependent than we think? Here I argue that the supposed incompatibility between these two rival but nevertheless overlapping design practices evokes deeper cultural conflicts that are themselves bolstered and sustained by profound social anxieties about gender and sexuality.

CONTESTED TERRITORIES

"Curtain Wars," the professional rivalries that cleave the interiors community, are not new; they date back at least to the eighteenth century. More often than not the interiors of upper-class dwellings were then outfitted not by the architects who designed them but by upholsterers—tradesmen who supervised the activities of skilled craftsmen including furniture makers and rug manufacturers. Referring to the friction that often resulted from this division of labor, many writers, including Nicolas le Camus de Mézières (in 1780) and William Mitford (in 1827), levied the same complaint: upholsterers corrupt the spatial integrity of buildings.[3] Such tensions came to a head in the late nine-

3. Le Camus de Mézières insisted that the furniture of an important bedchamber should be designed by the architect "and not by the upholsterer who should confine himself to executing the design"; William Mitford claimed that "the upholsterer's interest . . . is in direct opposition to the architect's credit." Peter Thornton recounts these, as well as other attacks against the upholsterer, in his *Authentic Décor: The Domestic Interior, 1620–1920* (New York: Viking, 1984).

teenth century when a new figure, the professional decorator, arrived on the scene, usurping the upholsterer's role. Hired to coordinate and assemble the elements of residential interiors, the first decorators were often amateurs, self-taught society women from prominent families, who, like novelist Edith Wharton and designer Elsie de Wolfe, shared their good taste with their affluent friends and peers. In *The Decoration of Houses* (1897), considered by many the first handbook for the modern interior decorator, Wharton observed the battle that pits architects against decorators. "As a result of this division of labor, house-decoration has ceased to be a branch of architecture," she wrote. "The upholsterer cannot be expected to have the preliminary training necessary for architectural work, and it is inevitable that in his hands form should be sacrificed to color and composition to detail . . . The confusion resulting from these unscientific methods has reflected itself in the lay mind, and house-decoration has come to be regarded as a black art by those who have seen their rooms subjected to the manipulations of the modern upholsterer."[4]

4. Edith Wharton and Ogden Codman Jr., *The Decoration of Houses* (New York: Classical America and Henry Hope Reed, 1997), xx.

By educating a new breed of design professionals "to understand the fundamental principles of their art," *The Decoration of Houses* would, Wharton hoped, bridge the already entrenched architect/decorator divide. Interestingly, the novelist collaborated on this guide with an architect, Ogden Codman Jr., who had helped her refurbish the interiors of her home in Newport, Rhode Island, and who later drafted the preliminary plans for the Mount, her villa in the Berkshires. But despite the cross-disciplinary intentions of the coauthors, in the end the text subordinates decoration to architecture. Wharton and Codman insist that "good decoration (which it must never be forgotten, is only interior architecture)" must obey the strictly architectural principles of logic, proportion, and decorum.[5] In many ways their

5. Wharton and Codman, *Decoration of Houses*, 13.

description of the ideal relationship between architect and decorator mirrors the relationship between turn-of-the-century affluent women and domestic space: while houses were presumed to be a female domain, housewives were ultimately subject to the authority of their home-owning husbands.[6]

6. But Wharton represents an exception to the paradigm: Vanessa Chase argues that Wharton's intellectual and economic independence allowed her to successfully invert typical gendered power relationships in the design of her own home, The Mount. See her "Edith Wharton, *The Decoration of Houses*, and Gender in Turn-of-the-Century America," in *Architecture and Feminism*, ed. Debra Coleman, Elizabeth Danzer, and Carol Henderson (New York: Princeton Architectural Press, 1996).

Since Wharton's era, not only have professional battle lines been drawn, but also architecture, whether viewed from the vantage of high or popular culture, seems always to emerge as the victor, commanding greater respect and prestige than does interior decoration. While the profession of interior decoration is scarcely a century old, the practice of furnishing the interiors of buildings is as old as the buildings themselves. Nevertheless, architecture has a long-studied history in the West (of monuments from the Parthenon to the Guggenheim, of architects from Ictinus to Frank Gehry), while interior decoration, conceived in this broader sense, has only since the late 1980s been considered worth serious scholarship. And even when art historians and museum curators acknowledge the legacy of interior design, they accord it a subordinate status. The very phrases "fine arts" and "decorative arts," used by art historians and museum curators to distinguish architecture from interior design, betray institutionalized prejudices. Such ostensibly innocent labels subtly but forcefully uphold the apparent superiority of architecture over interior design. Moreover, the structure of contemporary design education and professional licensing reinforces the disciplinary segregation authorized by scholars, dividing architecture and interior design into separate schools and departments, each with its own curriculum, degrees, and licenses.

Bridging high and popular culture, design journalism perpetuates what I am calling Curtain Wars. Mainstream shelter magazines and professional architectural journals reinforce the architect/decorator divide through the different ways interiors are written about, photographed, propped, and graphically presented. Shelter magazines shy away from describing the designer's overall spatial conception, preferring instead to concentrate on furniture and objects, while architecture magazines tend to present interiors eradicated of all traces of the decorator. These journalistic conventions confirm each profession's mutual suspicion of the other—the architect's belief that furniture compromises the integrity of the spatial concept, the decorator's conviction that the architectural shell is a backdrop for displaying valuable objects and furniture.

Yet despite the prejudices of educators, historians, and journalists, architecture and interior design inevitably intersect. The impulse to erect disciplinary hierarchies is a vain attempt to mask the overlapping, fluid nature of these two occupations. In practice, if not in theory, architecture and interior design do not so much oppose as presuppose each other.

How else do we explain architects like Richard Meier and Robert Stern picking fabrics and designing china, while interior designers like Thierry Despont and Steven Sills erect walls and install plumbing? Especially in cities like New York, where interiors comprise a major share of design practices, architects and decorators are often in direct competition. Articles in popular magazines counseling readers on whether to hire an architect or a decorator highlight the interchangeability and confused identities of the two professions in the eyes of the public. Common wisdom suggests (and some building regulations require) that if the project calls for relocating partitions, plumbing, and electrical wiring, then you need an architect; but if the job demands specifying freestanding furniture, fabrics, and finishes, you hire a decorator. But these distinct job descriptions break down in actual practice. Experienced architects understand that to maintain the integrity of their vision, they must select the furniture, fabrics, and objects. And savvy decorators, regularly called on to locate plumbing and wiring, routinely make architectural adjustments.

Perhaps the best evidence of the porous boundaries between architecture and decoration can be found in the work of those most responsible for erecting the borders in the first place—the early generation of modernist architects. As the literal separation between inside and outside

breaks down with the development of the transparent curtain wall, so too does the boundary between architect and interior decorator. And that quintessential invention of modern architecture, "built-in" furniture (a hybrid between architecture and freestanding furniture), underscores the difficulty of determining where one practice ends and the other begins.

The advent of the built-in reflects modernism's advocacy of the totally designed architectural interior, a notion that, ironically, coincides with the birth of the professional decorator at the turn of the century. Avant-garde architects like Charles Rennie Mackintosh, Frank Lloyd Wright, and Ludwig Mies van der Rohe insisted on the integration of architecture and interior design, and their domestic work comprised custom-designed furniture and accessories. The Belgian Art Nouveau architect Henry van de Velde even designed dresses for his clients so that they would harmonize with his decorative schemes. As modern architects claimed to distance themselves from what they considered the superficial excesses of decorators, they assumed many of the roles and responsibilities of the latter, a practice that persists today. Nevertheless, to recognize such masters of modern architecture as Frank Lloyd Wright and Le Corbusier as important "interior decorators" who contributed significantly to the history of interior design would, in some circles, be tantamount to denigrating their legacy. How can we account for this contradiction at the heart of modern architecture, a practice that regards interior design either as entirely external or entirely internal to itself?

Should the boundaries codified by practitioners and scholars be understood as the architecture profession's defensive response to the rise of the decorating profession? Does the marketplace require both architects and decorators to differentiate their identities so that they can vie for the same clients? While professional competition is

1
Mark Robbins, *Will, 49, Provincetown,* 2003. From the *Households* series.

surely an important factor, I believe that the roots of these professional rivalries run much deeper. Institutional prejudices and interdisciplinary disputes not only perpetuate Curtain Wars, they are also symptomatic of our deepest and most ingrained anxieties about the nature of masculinity, femininity, and homosexuality. Such disputes mirror the broad cultural assumptions that shape our impressions of both disciplines, as well as our ideas about the identities of the professionals who practice them.

ENGENDERING RESPECT

By identifying manliness with the genuine and womanliness with the artificial, the Western architectural tradition has for two millenniums associated the ornamented surface with femininity. Discussing the origins of Doric and Ionic columns, Vitruvius famously wrote: "In the invention of the two different kinds of columns, they borrowed manly beauty, naked and unadorned, for the one, and for the other the delicacy, adornment, and proportions characteristic of women."[7] For classical architects ornament was

7. Vitruvius, *The Ten Books on Architecture,* trans. Morris Hicky Morgan (New York: Dover, 1960), 104.

acceptable, provided it was properly subordinated to the tectonic logic of buildings, in much the same way women were taught to be subservient to men.

Of course, the status of ornament changed dramatically with the advent of modernism. Justifying their claim for an authentic, rational, and timeless architecture, architects like Adolf Loos and Le Corbusier enlisted gender prejudices in the quest to repudiate ornament, which they considered extraneous to buildings, potentially corrupting their formal integrity. Evoking ornament's longstanding and pejorative association with femininity, these architects preferred stripped-down buildings, which they compared to "naked men," over ornamented structures, which they likened to overdressed women. They found their archetypal model in the image of the male nude ("naked and unadorned"), the

very antithesis of the female masquerader, embellished with clothes and makeup.[8]

8. See Mary McLeod, "Undressing Architecture: Fashion, Gender, and Modernity," and Mark Wigley, "White Out: Fashioning the Modern," in *Architecture: In Fashion*, ed. Deborah Fausch et al. (New York: Princeton Architectural Press, 1994). Mark Wigley's *White Walls, Designer Dresses: The Fashioning of Modern Architecture* (Cambridge: MIT Press, 1995) discusses in depth the ambivalent but nonetheless pivotal role fashion played in the discourse of modern architecture.

The modernist argument against exterior ornament, based on its metaphorical resemblance to fashion, becomes even more extreme when brought to bear on the interior, where decoration becomes conflated with clothing.[9] Another

9. Here I am elaborating on the notion of "architectural dressing" discussed in the introduction to the collection of essays I edited, *Stud: Architectures of Masculinity* (New York: Princeton Architectural Press, 1996).

term for curtains, "window dressing," with its allusion to apparel, underscores the intimate association of interior decoration with fashion and femininity. Like drapery on mannequins, drapes on windows "outfit" the domestic interior. While ornament, designed by architects, is typically materially and conceptually consistent with a building's skin, the fabrics and curtains selected by decorators are independent elements detachable from architectural surfaces. Draped with fabrics and finery, the decorated room calls to mind the decorated woman whose allure derives from superficial adornment—"womanliness as masquerade."[10] In *Women as Decoration,* written in 1917, Emily

10. The phrase was coined by psychoanalyst Joan Riviere, herself a dressmaker before writing the famous 1929 essay "Womanliness as a Masquerade." See Victor Burgin, James Donald, and Cora Kaplan, eds., *Formations of Fantasy* (London and New York: Methuen, 1986), 35–44.

Burbank makes explicit this analogy between interior design and female costume, counseling women on how to dress in harmony with their surroundings. "Woman," she observed, "is an important factor in the decorative scheme of any setting—the vital spark to animate the interior decoration, private or public."[11]

11. Emily Burbank, *Women as Decoration* (New York: Dodd, Mead and Company, 1917).

Burbank's equation of women with decoration coincides with another historical development: the promotion of decorating as a woman's vocation. While architecture has, until recently, been considered an occupation of men and for men, interior design has, since its inception, been viewed as a practice if not always of women then certainly for women. "We take it for granted," Elsie de Wolfe wrote in 1913, "that this American home is always the woman's home . . . It is the personality of the mistress that the home expresses. Men are forever guests in our homes, no matter how much happiness they may find there."[12]

12. Elsie de Wolfe, *The House in Good Taste* (New York: Century Company, 1913).

It took a confluence of new historical forces—industrialization and the rise of the bourgeois family—to consolidate ancient prejudices and to transform interior design into a women's field. The notion of the domestic interior as predominantly a female domain, a concept often taken for granted, is, in fact, of recent origin, for historically the domestic household was associated with patriarchy. Aristocratic estates and their contents were passed down through generations of male heirs; they were the tangible signs of family wealth, power, and prestige. Throughout the nineteenth century, two linked factors profoundly altered this centuries-old tradition. The rise of industrialism made possible the manufacture of furniture. And the decline of the aristocracy and the rise of a socially mobile bourgeoisie created a new consumer, the housewife, whose role it was to purchase and arrange the commodities her husband no longer inherited.[13]

13. Two books that survey premodern developments are Mario Praz, *An Illustrated History of Interior Decoration* (New York: Thames and Hudson, 1982), and Peter Thornton, *Authentic Décor: The Domestic Interior, 1620–1920* (New York: Viking, 1984). For a discussion of the invention of the modern professional decorator, see "The Emergence of Interior Decoration as a Profession" in Ann Massey, *Interior Design of the 20th Century* (London: Thames and Hudson, 1990).

Feminist historians have exhaustively examined the impact of the gendered division of labor on domestic space. They have shown how, as the workplace became separated from the home in the nineteenth century and the domestic interior became the precinct of the housewife, a popular literature devoted to interior decorating emerged, geared to the female homemaker. Decorating, a practice once conducted by male architects and upholsterers, was thus appropriated by women—either by "do-it-yourself" housewives or by decorators, many of whom, like Elsie de Wolfe or Edith Wharton, were from wealthy, prominent families.

Professional status mirrors gender status: the subordinate relationship of interior decoration can be linked to its reputation as a woman's pastime. Not surprisingly, at the same time that nineteenth-century economic developments transformed both women and the domestic spaces they presided over into signifiers of male wealth, financial forces finally gave interior decoration its due. Widespread affluence in the early twentieth century fueled a burgeoning new market for home furnishings, a market encouraged by the popular press and geared to female consumers, which continues to expand today.

Given that curtains and other interior accouterments have recently become big business, it could be argued that popular journalism now champions decoration over architecture, regularly showcasing domestic design in such venues as the *New York Times* "House & Home" section and *Martha Stewart Living*. And given also the strong affinities between fashion and interior design, it is no wonder that decorating has become a staple feature of the fashion press. Often produced by the same publishing house (for instance, Condé Nast or Hearst) and sold side by side on the newsstands, fashion and shelter magazines sometimes feature the same stories and in certain cases, like *Vogue* and *House & Garden*, mirror each other graphically as well.

Disciplinary boundaries have become blurred beyond the pages of women's magazines. Stylists scout hip interiors as locations for fashion shoots, while top designers like

2

Mark Robbins, *Joan and Bob, Quogue, Long Island*, 2003. From the *Households* series.

Calvin Klein, Donna Karan, and Giorgio Armani (not to mention mass-market companies like Banana Republic) have begun to produce lines of home furnishings to complement the "lifestyle" cued by their clothes. Fashion designers have thus shrewdly colonized a branch of design more closely affiliated with architecture. Have architects ceded a lucrative market to clothing designers because decorating is still tainted by its associations with fashion and femininity? Perhaps. But there is no doubt that during the 1990s, the cultural currency of fashion rose dramatically. The recent alliance between Prada and the Pritzker Prize winners Rem Koolhaas and Herzog and de Meuron suggests that, on the contrary, architects may finally be ready to relinquish their longstanding suspicions of fashion and decoration.

ENTER THE GAY DECORATOR

Curtain Wars implicate more than sex and gender; they also participate in the cultural construction of sexuality. Scenes from two Hollywood films, for example, the 1949 adaptation of Ayn Rand's *The Fountainhead* and *Any Wednesday,* made in 1966, both reinforce the age-old image of the "macho" male architect; simultaneously, they fine-tune a newer cultural cliché—the gay interior decorator.

In *The Fountainhead,* Howard Roark, as played by Gary Cooper, personifies the architect as the epitome of masculinity. In the climactic trial scene, Roark defends himself for dynamiting his own project rather than seeing it disfigured by collaborating designers; the concept of masculinity is at the heart of his self-defense. A real man, says Roark, refuses to compromise his integrity and independence; the architect must follow his own vision rather than capitulate to the client's whim. In the final moments of the movie, Roark's adoring wife is conveyed upward by a construction elevator to the top of his latest project—a high-rise, of course—where he awaits her. Throughout the scene the camera's mobile eye is fixed worshipfully on Roark,

who stands atop and indeed seems to surmount the skyscraper—an image that literally conflates the architect with manhood.

In *The Fountainhead,* professional identity is reinforced too by sartorial style. The clean lines of Howard Roark's dark suits, echoing the simple geometry of his buildings, indicate his heterosexual manliness. Similarly, in *Any Wednesday,* in a scene in which the male decorator consults with the newlywed played by Jane Fonda, the silk handkerchief that accessorizes his blazer betrays not only his design sensibility but also his sexual identity. And his flamboyant speech and gestures (which match the outrageous fees he freely admits to charging) call up the ubiquitous but suspect stereotype of the gay interior decorator.

If the history of the professional decorator has been neglected, the subject of homosexuality and interior decoration has been largely ignored.[14] Interestingly enough, two of

14. One of the few authors to address the prominent role of gay and lesbian practitioners in interior design is Aaron Betsky, who takes up this topic in *Queer Space: Architecture and Same-Sex Desire* (New York: William Morrow, 1997).

the field's earliest and most influential members—Edith Wharton's collaborator Ogden Codman and his contemporary Elsie de Wolfe—were both homosexuals. A review of Codman's work in *Architectural Record* criticizes his interior designs for gaining "variety at the expense of virility."[15]

15. "Some Recent Works by Ogden Codman Jr.," *Architectural Record*, July 1905, 51.

While historians have described how decorating came to be considered a woman's pastime, they have yet to account for its emergence as a gay profession. One likely explanation is that interior design—like two allied design fields, fashion and theater—attracts a disproportionate number of gay men because gay men, already marginalized for their apparent femininity, are less reluctant to assume occupations that have traditionally been deemed feminine. But it is hardly coincidental that interior design, much like fashion and theater, is a discipline invested in the notion of self-fashioning through artifice. Borrowing the useful concept developed by feminist and queer theorists of sexual identity as "performance," I have argued elsewhere that architecture participates in the staging of individual identity.[16]

16. See Sanders, *Stud*, 11–25; reprinted in this volume.

According to this view, masculinity and femininity are constructed through the repetition of culturally prescribed norms, including gestures, mannerisms, clothing. Daily life resembles theater, a stage where men and women learn to act culturally sanctioned roles. Extending this analogy, we can compare interiors to stage sets that, along with costumes and props, help actors create convincing portrayals. Because of their outsider status, many gay men, like women, are acutely aware of the performative nature of human subjectivity. Could it be that this awareness, which some consider a survival instinct, allows gay men to be unusually well represented in decorating, a craft in which applied surfaces—fabrics, wallpapers, paint colors—are manipulated in order to fashion personality?

The idea that interiors express human and in particular feminine identity is a message reiterated in periodicals like *House Beautiful* and *Metropolitan Home*. Like apparel, decor discloses the secrets of selfhood. Perhaps the most exaggerated and paradoxical examples of this staple of design journalism are photo spreads showcasing celebrity homes. Inviting readers to identify with the camera's voyeuristic eye, magazines like *Architectural Digest, Vanity Fair,* and *In Style* urge us to peek into the homes of stars like Madonna and Cher. Suspending disbelief, we momentarily delude ourselves into believing that these contrived and often outré environments reliably mirror the authentic selves of their occupants.

Patrons have long looked to designers to outfit both themselves and their homes to communicate self-image to the outside world; but the rich and famous are not the only ones savvy enough to understand the importance of a well-

appointed home. Since the nineteenth century, publications aimed largely at middle-class women have instructed amateurs on how to fashion themselves and their domestic environments to reflect who they are or aspire to be. With the feminization of the bourgeois home comes a new conception of the domestic interior: a unique abode that mirrors the temperament of its (female) homemaker. Taste, once considered an expression of class and breeding but now freed from its aristocratic associations, thus becomes understood as an expression of personality. Following a literary model established by architectural theorists from Vitruvius to Laugier, two early and influential decorating texts—Wharton and Codman's *The Decoration of Houses* and de Wolfe's *The House in Good Taste*—counsel readers that decorating, much like architectural design, is essentially a rational process, based not upon whim or whimsy but rather upon objective principles. But as the genre of the decorating book evolved during the twentieth century, a contrary tendency emerged, one that sought to distance interior design from architectural precedent. Two popular books written by designers known for working with celebrity clients—Dorothy Draper and Billy Baldwin—illustrate this trend by upholding womanly taste, not manly reason, as a prerequisite for practice. Both counsel women on how to express themselves through decor.[17]

17. Counseling female readers, Draper writes: "Your home is the backdrop of your life, whether it is a palace or a one-room apartment. It should be honestly your own—an expression of your personality. So many people stick timidly to the often-uninspired conventional ideas or follow some expert's methods slavishly. Either way they are more or less living in someone else's house." Dorothy Draper, *Decorating Is Fun! How to Be Your Own Decorator* (New York: Doubleday, Dovan, 1941), 4; Billy Baldwin, *Billy Baldwin Remembers* (New York: Harcourt Brace Jovanovich, 1974).

It might be expected that this subjective design approach would make interior designers unnecessary: consult your inner decorator rather than hire a professional. However, as Draper's and Baldwin's texts both demonstrate, decorators quickly learned to take advantage of this union

3

Mark Robbins, *American Philosophy, Nancy, 42, Mark, 51, Newton Highlands, Massachusetts,* 2003. From the *Households* series. Courtesy Nancy Bauer.

of decor and "womanly intuition," employing professional empathy as a strategy to distinguish themselves from "arrogant" male architects reputedly indifferent to client needs. Unlike stubborn architects who willfully impose their own ideas and values on patrons, the ideal decorator is a facilitator. According to Baldwin, "A decorator must first consider the kind of people for whom he works, how they lived, and their stated budget. Then, and only then, can he execute their wishes and requirements according to the best of his trained taste and experience."[18] Capitalizing on a

18. Baldwin, *Billy Baldwin Remembers*, 73.

seemingly innate ability to forge close and familiar client relationships, some decorators even came to resemble psychics, mediums who enabled housewives to channel their inner selves through their domestic furnishings.

True to the genre of decorating literature, both Draper and Baldwin gloss over a fundamental contradiction posed by their endorsement of the intuitive creator: the attempt to teach skills that ultimately cannot be taught. Moreover, although both authors claim to disavow the "signature designer," the books ultimately validate this figure. Peppered with personal anecdotes, both volumes double as publicity memoirs. Ignoring the incontrovertible fact that people hire decorators precisely because they believe that "taste" can be purchased, Draper and Baldwin strive to convince the reader that hiring a famous designer will result in self-actualization.

Despite the sex of their authors, the subliminal portrait of the decorator painted in both these interior-design books is of a female, thus playing into two of Western culture's long-standing associations with femininity: artifice, fabricated through the application of adornment, and subterfuge (while apparently submissive, women ultimately get their way by creating the illusion that others are in control). Not necessarily oppressive and limiting, these stereotypes have sometimes proved professionally beneficial. Under the

right circumstances, the reputation of the cooperative and feminized decorator, when opposed to the figure of the domineering and unsympathetic architect, can pay off. ("I don't build for clients," say Howard Roark. "I get clients in order to build.") The gay male decorator's intimacy with his female patrons—coupled with his first-hand understanding of the crucial role interiors play in human self-fashioning—permits him to be trusted, to become, in a sense, "just one of the girls."

ENTER THE EMASCULATED ARCHITECT

The popular perception of interior decorating as inherently feminine, conducted by either women or effeminate gay men, not only accounts for the field's inferior status, it also effectively threatens the self-esteem of many architects. For some practitioners, the unstable borders separating architecture from interior design touch directly on the vulnerability that lies at the core of manhood. Whether seen from the vantage of psychoanalytic theory or cultural history, masculinity, while seemingly invincible, is fragile.[19] Architects are inevitably asked to perform certain

19. Although they offer different explanations, both cultural historians and psychoanalytic theorists argue that modern masculinity is in crisis. Historians attribute this to the aftermath of World War II, when traditional roles in both the workplace and the home were transformed. See Michael S. Kimmel, "Consuming Manhood: The Feminization of American Culture and the Recreation of the Male Body, 1832–1920," in *The Male Body: Features, Destinies, Exposures*, ed. Lawrence Goldstein (Ann Arbor: University of Michigan Press, 1994), 12–41. For a psychoanalytic reading of masculinity as masquerade, see Kaja Silverman, *Male Subjectivity at the Margins* (New York and London: Routledge, 1992). Several recent books explore the crisis of masculinity in terms of the depriving yet felt-to-be-necessary distance boys create from their mothers in order to feel like independent, "masculine" beings, a distance girls feel less need for. See, for instance, *The Reproduction of Mothering*, by Nancy Chodorow; *In a Time of Fallen Heros*, by William Betcher and William S. Pollock; and *I Don't Want to Talk About It*, by Terrence Real.

"decorating" activities—like picking furniture and fabrics—that call into question their manliness. Already insecure about their attraction to tasks that society deems unmanly, for some practitioners the architectural profession represents a strange sort of closet, a refuge that allows them (albeit with some discomfort) to engage in practices considered otherwise unacceptable for "real" men. Still, many architects feel they must defend against the sneaking suspicion that inside every architect lurks a decorator. Ultimately, architects disavow interior design as a way of overcompensating for masculine vulnerability; they are compelled to draw emphatic limits between two professions whose contours inevitably overlap.

Today, with interior design finally beginning to receive greater professional and cultural recognition, Curtain Wars underscore the collective low self-esteem of the architectural profession, exacerbating the male architect's doubts about his self-determination and -empowerment. The cultural priority accorded to architecture over interior design was never all that secure. Despite the grand historical narratives promoted by art historians, architecture, although an ancient craft, is nevertheless a relatively new profession that has struggled for respect. To this day architects fight to overcome their image as aristocratic amateurs.[20] Unable to

20. While we have come to view architecture as a venerable and hence respectable practice, we must not forget that the professional standing of the architect is a relatively recent invention. During the Middle Ages, architects belonged to guilds and were considered artisans. While the names of some master builders have been recorded for posterity, it was not until the Renaissance that the status of architects, along with that of artists, was elevated from anonymous craftsmen to individual creators. Even then, professional recognition did not come quickly. From the Renaissance through the mid-nineteenth century, architecture was still considered an "art" largely practiced by amateurs like Thomas Jefferson, who personified the self-taught "gentleman architect." Not until the establishment of academies like the École des Beaux-Arts in Paris in the nineteenth century did architects define themselves as experts who learn not on the job but in school, a change in status that led to the licensing of professional architects in the early twentieth century.

convince the public that architects provide indispensable skills, architecture is often viewed as an expendable luxury. Why hire an architect when many states allow clients to enlist professional engineers or contractors to do the job? Although they endure similarly lengthy training and demanding apprenticeships, architects typically command significantly lower fees than do other professionals—doctors, lawyers, and yes, even interior designers. And while the public image of the architect is as a dashing and sometimes even celebrated figure, rarely does this positive appeal translate into actual value in the marketplace.

To add personal insult to this economic injury, architects often find themselves, despite their reputations for machismo, disempowered by colleagues and clients alike. The architect's expertise is often challenged both by those for whom he works—clients, developers, institutions—and by those who work for him—structural engineers, contractors, construction workers, and even decorators. (An interesting example of the age-old feud between architect and decorator involved Richard Meier and Thierry Despont at the new Getty Museum in Los Angeles. Perhaps what proved so humiliating for Meier was not just that he was forced to compromise the integrity of his pristine galleries with "bordello-red" damask wall coverings, retro tapestries, dentilated cornices, and plastic moldings but also that the infringement of the "suave" society decorator signified Meier's ultimate loss of control. But the real battle took place not between decorator and architect but between architect and client, the museum director John Walsh, who hired Despont in the first place. Contrary to the myth of the domineering architect, it is still the client who holds the purse strings and, ultimately, the power.) In recent years a crisis of confidence has overtaken the architectural profession. As buildings become more complicated and expensive, architects have been "relieved" of many of the technical responsibilities they once fulfilled: specialists now handle engineering, structural, and construction issues. Often in the case of large-scale projects like high-rise buildings, developers retain signature architects like Michael Graves who function as glorified styling consultants, hired to create skins—building facades and lobby decor—for structures designed by others. Some attribute this development to Philip Johnson, who was hired by

4
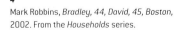
Mark Robbins, *Bradley, 44, David, 45, Boston,* 2002. From the *Households* series.

Donald Trump in 1995 to style the exterior of the former Gulf and Western Building, now rebuilt as the Trump International Hotel and Tower.[21] But surely the architect as skin doctor

21. Tracie Rozhon, "Condos on the Rise, by Architectural Stars," *New York Times*, July 19, 2001.

dates further back, to postmodernism in the early 1980s. Transferring the logic of retail to buildings, developers like Trump acknowledge the cachet, prestige, and media attention associated with celebrity designers. In today's global marketplace, high-profile architectural practices are rapidly dismantling the once-firm boundaries between architect, decorator, and fashion stylist.

Yet in a world in which non-celebrity architects are increasingly marginalized by the public and by their peers, it is no wonder that many architects might find picking upholstery and curtains threatening, this seemingly inconsequential activity tainted by its deep-seated associations with women and homosexuality. Today, however, as restrictive gender roles have become more flexible and alternative modes of sexuality are more openly expressed, professional possibilities are emerging—possibilities that portend the transcendence of the architecture/decorator divide. Not only are women now encouraged to be both high-powered professionals and nurturing mothers, but men are also increasingly permitted to express themselves through activities once closed off—they are free to be both athletes and aesthetes, breadwinners and homemakers. And decorating is finally coming out of the closet. Not only are shelter magazines showcasing domestic interiors inhabited by same-sex couples (who are often decorators), but professional journals like *Interior Design* also run provocative homo-social advertisements directed at both female and gay designers. Interestingly, the belated but nevertheless welcome acknowledgment by journalists of the significant role that gays play in the design community coincides with an even more striking development: mainstream compa-

nies like the *New York Times, Wallpaper,* and even Ikea are setting their sights on a new household consumer—straight men hip to the latest decorating trends. In "Pulls and Pillowcases: It's a Man's World," a *New York Times* article devoted to how this burgeoning tendency has created new tensions between cohabiting men and women, journalist Rick Marin writes, "There are two kinds of men. The kind that spend long hours lying on the couch in front of professional wrestling. And those of us who prefer to spend our spare time shopping for the perfect couch to lie on. You'd think women would prefer to cohabit with the shopping man. Not necessarily."[22]

22. Rick Marin, "Pulls and Pillowcases: It's a Man's World," *New York Times*, February 8, 2001, F:1.

Now that mainstream culture is finally beginning to accept the fluidity of gender identities, both architects and decorators are able to embrace one of the best aspects of domestic design: its ability to realign activities once conventionally designated as distinctly "masculine" or "feminine"—science and art, logic and intuition, architecture and interior decoration. Professionals who can integrate such supposedly opposite skills are newly empowered to question conventional and restrictive notions of gender and to invent a new design vocabulary that will merge the best features of the divided worlds of architecture and decoration. Collapsing various distinctions—between building scale and human scale, stable shell and freestanding furniture—interior decoration and architecture will finally be understood as continuous practices. Whether rigid or malleable, found on the inside or the outside, the cladding that sheathes the surfaces of our buildings works like the clothing that covers our bodies; both are coded to enable us to articulate the various identities we assume every day. The time is ripe for a new generation of designers to move beyond Curtain Wars and invent a hybrid design vocabulary that will allow a range of human identities and activities to transpire in domestic space.

ADAPTED FROM *HARVARD DESIGN MAGAZINE* 16 (WINTER/SPRING 2002). MANY OF THE THEMES AND ISSUES EXPLORED HERE WERE RAISED IN THE "CURTAIN WARS" CONFERENCE I ORGANIZED AT PARSONS SCHOOL OF DESIGN IN 1997.

ERGOTECTONICS: THE MULTI-IDENTITY/ MULTI-TASK ENVIRONMENT

Today, homes provide shelter not only for nuclear families but also for single parents, same-sex couples, men and women living alone, and roommates. At the same time telecommunications—computers, faxes, cell phones—have decentralized the workplace and ushered in new economies that have made working at home a viable option. While we pay lip service to each of these social and technological issues separately, we tend to forget that they are interrelated and mutually reinforcing cultural developments with significant architectural ramifications. In short, homes have become multi-identity, multi-task environments. Over the course of a single day, men and women alike are not only called on to assume a variety of domestic and professional roles—as partners, parents, and wage earners—but often to do so in the same domestic space.

Architecture lags far behind these rapid social developments. Why do we at the start of a new millennium consent to occupy dwellings designed to meet the living requirements of households depicted in 1960s sitcoms? While contemporary architects often complain that developers build new houses masquerading as old ones, even more troubling is the gap between layout and lifestyle. Perpetuating midcentury domestic ideals whose origins date back to the nineteenth century, ordinary developer plans subtly but powerfully prescribe obsolete hierarchical gender relationships and puritanical ideas about propriety.[1]

1. By now feminist and cultural historians have charted the development of the bourgeois house, showing how its design both reflected and helped shape economic and gender relationships by spatializing a conception of living and working in which each takes place in an autonomous "sphere," a conception we today understand as stemming from a nineteenth-century notion of domesticity. For the most part, men, as wage earners, were assigned to the public urban realm, while women, as household managers, were relegated to the private domestic realm. But it was not until the postwar era, when automobiles and highway networks became available to the middle classes, that the nineteenth-century domestic dream became a reality in the American suburb.

Built with the presumption that they will be occupied by nuclear families, these formulaic dwellings isolate people and functions by rigidly separating public spaces (living and dining rooms) from private spaces (bedrooms and bathrooms). Reproducing an outmoded division between work and leisure, designers seem unaware that people other than housewives increasingly work at home. When the conflation between public and private space is acknowledged, designers assume that the traditional house need only be subtly adapted to accommodate the new media technologies that make a house an office. Thus, we are expected to rely on stores like Ikea, where we can purchase equipment and accessories like desks and computer carts, to retrofit freshly built dens and second bedrooms into do-it-yourself home offices.

Contrary to expectation, this outmoded way of thinking about the contemporary domestic program also informs custom-designed homes based on modernist residential planning principles. Despite the promise of the free plan, modern masters like Mies van de Rohe and Frank Lloyd Wright accepted and reproduced the normative social conventions already inscribed in the conventional bourgeois house, segregating private spaces like bedrooms and bathrooms as well as service areas like kitchens and servants' quarters into separate wings. Moreover, with the exception of artists' studios, residential working quarters are few and far between in modern architecture. Modern architects transferred their obsession with functional differentiation from micro to macro, drafting urban plans that cordon off residential and commercial zones.

Despite their predilection for programmatic segregation, modern architects did employ open plans in places where they would meet with little social resistance: public living areas. This legacy persists today, not only in high-end homes designed by architects but also in developer homes that frequently collapse cooking, dining, and living into one large open space, the " family room." Yet then as now, even when related functions are allowed to coexist in the same space, furniture assumes the responsibility that walls and partitions once did, fixing spatial identities through furniture groupings. Living and dining "areas" replace formal living and dining "rooms."

Today, as the boundaries between masculine and feminine, living and working, and public and private space become more porous, homes can no longer afford to function as single-family, single-purpose environments. Instead, dwellings have become miniature worlds that, although limited in scale, are hooked into vast global networks. And as dwellings become stages that facilitate a diverse range of human performances, they must come well equipped for rapid changes of scene. For example, a work-at-home single parent requires a domestic environment where he or she can quickly shift back and forth between personal and professional roles, a multi-task environment for both meal preparation and client reports. The relationship between human identity and spatial identity is reciprocal: each presupposes the other. If who we are is defined by human actions performed in space, then we increasingly require homes as flexible as our identities.

Our quick-change lifestyles require living spaces that challenge the ingrained preconceptions of design professionals, architects and decorators alike. When they take on residential commissions, architects, who until recently were mostly men, typically design the building envelope. Working with fixed elements, they consider questions of site, massing, and infrastructure as they impact the overall distribution of rooms. Then, more often than not, women or professional decorators outfit the hard stable shell created by architects with more ephemeral elements like fabrics and furniture geared to the more specific and intimate needs of the human body. Each discipline compensates for the omissions of the other: architects attend to large-scale issues while decorators account for human-scale needs. Clearly these oppositions between exterior and interior,

hard and soft, macro and micro draw on deep-seated stereotypes of masculinity and femininity that continue to shape our underlying impression of domestic environments as well as of the design professionals who create them.

Devising domestic environments that promote fluid domestic identities depends on inventing a new design vocabulary that merges the best aspects of the divided worlds of architecture and decoration. Merging materials and techniques from each discipline, designers must learn to integrate both the pliable materials favored by decorators and the durable materials employed by architects. Bringing togéther the best of both worlds, designers must invent a hybrid formal language that, bridging building and human scales, allows a diverse range of human activities to transpire in coterminous spaces.

Shedding domestic preconceptions also entails embracing an expanded notion of multipurpose space. Despite their ostensibly divergent design perspectives, the fixed rooms designed by the architect and the freestanding furniture placed within them by decorators are both assigned more or less stable uses. But today's homeowners, often faced with floor areas as modest as their budgets, are increasingly looking to designers to help them squeeze maximum use out of minimum floor space. Furniture, not architecture, comes to the rescue—but not without a certain level of anxiety. Daybeds, Murphy beds, and sofa beds convert studio apartments, living rooms, and dens into private sleeping quarters.[2] While acknowledging adaptability,

2. Obviously, the market for these contraptions is driven by the concept of the private bedroom, a space we now take for granted, even though it is relatively new in the history of Western domestic architecture. Until the eighteenth century, designers felt no compunction to disguise beds, which they treated as elaborately decorated wooden structures that held their own in multipurpose public rooms. Even with the invention of quarters reserved for sleeping, people as important as Louis XIV regularly received guests in their bedchambers. (See Witold Rybczynski, *Home: A Short History of an Idea*, New York: Penguin Books, 1987.) But today, the bedroom is an exclusively private domain. Whether responding to notions of privacy, propriety, or class, the driving force behind convertible beds is shame—the need to conceal an unsightly private act forced to unfold (literally) in public space.

these space-saving design strategies still cling to the notion of invariable identity. For example, the convertible sofa, as well as the room it was designed to transform, oscillates between two fixed uses: sofa/living room on the one hand and bed/bedroom on the other. Yet somehow the sofa is never attractive enough, the bed is never comfortable enough, and the makeshift guest room falls short of the bedroom it replicates. Never measuring up to the furniture or the room it was intended to approximate, convertibles in the end always seem to draw attention to the flaws—lack of space, comfort, and wealth—that they were invented to conceal.

Moving beyond the useful, but nonetheless limited notion of "convertibility," I propose Ergotectonics, domestic environments with polymorphous identities. Erasing hard and fast distinctions between architecture and decoration, built-ins and freestanding furniture, these open-ended landscapes will encourage simultaneous uses, allowing their occupants to freely shift roles and activities. Designers need only take common, if intuitive household practices as their guide: objects intended for single functions are often used in unintended and multiple ways. Most everyone living in a cramped apartment uses the kitchen table as a home office, the underside of the bed as a storage closet. But at the same time, domestic spaces and the activities they sponsor are not always interchangeable. Activities like food preparation, bathing, and working require particular spatial conditions and equipment. Ergotectonics would wrestle with the contradictory demands of generic and specific use.

This reconciliation demands fresh ways of organizing domestic programs. Rather than arranging dwellings according to rooms identified with single purposes (kitchens for cooking, bedrooms for sleeping), we must invent a new household taxonomy that conceives of residential space as an interconnected series of networks—surfaces, materials, and infrastructures—that connect overlapping activities traditionally viewed as distinct from one another. Consider, for a moment, the hard, horizontal surfaces within the home that link a variety of activities. Both dining and working are served by elements—tabletops and desktops—calibrated to the height of the seated body. Likewise, preparing food and putting on makeup, cleaning vegetables and brushing teeth are all actions performed against standing-height waterproof counters. Pliable upholstered surfaces adapted to the contours of seated or reclining bodies are another common element in almost every room of the house. Yet fabrics are, for the most part, used only for furnishings that are considered single-purpose entities, independent from the hard building shell that encloses them. Flouting design conventions, why not regard both work surfaces and upholstered surfaces as dynamic multifunctional systems that weave their way through all the spaces of the home?

As we acquire more and more products and equipment for work and leisure, storage becomes another infrastructure central to the contemporary dwelling. Traditionally, designers address storage requirements through differentiation, either concealing belongings behind closed doors (closets) or creating freestanding elements (cabinets) geared for specific rooms. But while they might vary in dimension, storage elements like broom and coat closets or kitchen and file cabinets are, in the end, all compartments for categorizing commodities. Instead of isolating different types of products in use-specific spaces, designers should treat storage as a continuous network that serves an overlapping series of multifunctional spaces.

Storage is not the only closeted domestic infrastructure. Out of sight and out of mind, pipes, wires, and ducts concealed in wall and ceiling cavities cater to the needs of the biological body. HVAC systems (heating, ventilating, air-conditioning) ensure comfortable atmospheric conditions. Plumbing typically stems from a central service core and joins kitchens, bathrooms, and other wet zones of the house. In plan, these spaces dedicated to corporeal needs are often located adjacent to each other for reasons of economy and efficiency. Yet disavowing the link between eating and elimination, social convention dictates that these proximate spaces are rarely allowed to spatially or visually overlap: the naked and abject body must be screened from view. As we gradually lift taboos about sex and the corporeal body, dwelling design will allow kitchens and bathrooms to communicate, expressing the link between two spaces that use water and waterproof materials to wash and dress food and bodies alike.

Another hidden infrastructure, electricity, plays an increasingly crucial role in domestic design as technological devices infiltrate every facet of our lives. Historically, household appliances, like refrigerators and stoves, and electronics, like televisions and hi-fi systems, functioned as activity-generating hubs that resulted in spatial differentiation—kitchens, offices, dens. As affordable televisions became mass-marketed in the 1950s, sets came to compete with, if not replace, the hearth as the center of the home, a development that influenced house plans and even living room furniture arrangements.[3] No longer one-of-a-

3. Lyn Spiegel discusses the impact of television on midcentury domestic space planning in "The Suburban Home Companion: Television and the Neighborhood Idea in Postwar America," in *Sexuality and Space*, ed. Beatriz Colomina (New York: Princeton Architectural Press, 1992), 185–217.

kind objects that centralize activities, appliances today have become networked. We put televisions, VCRs, stereo systems, computers, and sometimes even kitchen appliances in more than one (and sometimes every) room of the home. And yet the construction industry still builds dwellings that are electronically challenged, falling far short of the complex demands placed on our increasingly wired lives.

In fact, our homes now require the electrical accessibility that we once expected only from the workplace: outlets on all available surfaces, walls, floors, and ceilings. What to do? Homes might employ accessible floors, systems borrowed from commercial office design. Applying the concept of the dropped ceiling to the floor, these suspended systems define a cavity that allows wiring to be run to any location. As wireless technologies become readily available, perhaps this problem will be less acute in the future.

Domestic design has already begun to follow the lead of product design. In the same way that equipment from exercise bikes to toaster ovens is internally digitized, tectonic surfaces, equipped with built-in computer chips, will also soon become "smart." Floors, walls, ceilings, and counters will not support electronic devices, they will become such devices. The myriad appliances, gadgets, and wires that currently clutter our homes will be eliminated, and electronic devices, many of them wireless, will eventually be seamlessly integrated within the horizontal and vertical surfaces of dwellings.

Relinquishing deep-seated preconceptions about privacy, propriety, and the body, Ergotectonics views the home as an integrated network of overlapping surfaces and connected infrastructures: durable waterproof multitask work counters suitable for working, preparing meals, and casual dining; resilient upholstered elements that sponsor lounging, entertaining, exercising, and sleeping; storage units designed to accommodate everything from canned goods to clothing; wet areas that cater to the intimate needs of the biological body—cooking, eating, washing, dressing—without pandering to traditional notions of decency; "smart" walls and counters outfitted with integrated digital and electronic devices. Finding a common ground between the rival worlds of architecture and decoration, Ergotectonics promises highly articulate domestic landscapes that will allow each of us to perform our daily rituals in flexible environments responsive to our fluid lives.

ADAPTED FROM *INSIDE SPACE: EXPERIMENTS IN REDEFINING ROOMS* (CAMBRIDGE: MIT LIST VISUAL ARTS CENTER, 2001).

VITALE LOFT NEW YORK, NEW YORK, 1999–2000

In many ways, apartment design in New York City is dependent on plumbing. The location of plumbing stacks often dictates the placement of kitchens and bathrooms, which are in many cases adjoined. Propriety typically leads designers to disguise the uncomfortable proximity of these two related spaces that register our culture's deepest and most profound anxieties about sexuality, abjection, and the corporeal body.

In the Vitale loft, we chose to celebrate rather than disguise the proximity of these two pivotal domestic spaces by consolidating all domestic programs associated with water and bodily functions into one concrete core. Bathroom and kitchen, although bisected by a translucent glass privacy screen, are linked by a continuous, poured, waterproof concrete surface, allowing them to freely overlap. The client, either alone or with friends, can dine, lounge, or bathe, moving freely between kitchen, bath, and bedroom.

Our design for the Vitale loft maximizes spatial and programmatic flexibility while also creating an environment that caters to the tactile body. As we spend more of our time navigating virtual space in the digital realm, the claims of the sensuous body become more important than ever.

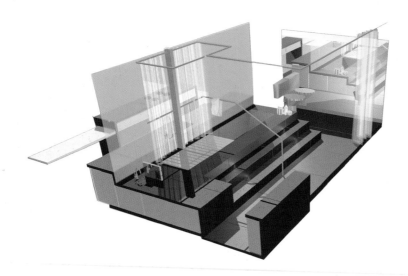

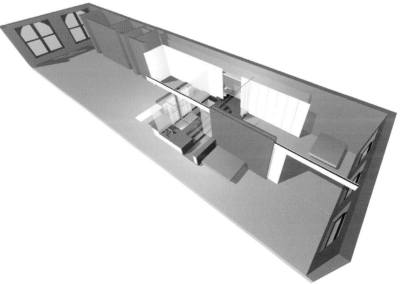

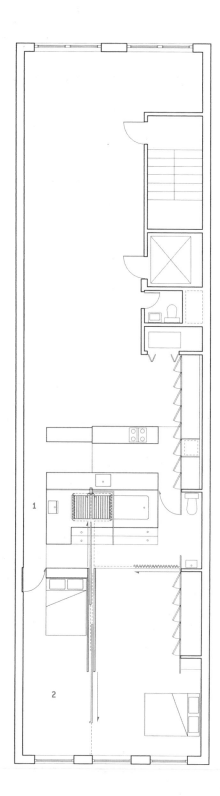

1
Guest Sink
A hinged door in the plumbing island reveals a guest sink embedded in the concrete core.

2
Guest Bedroom
Concealed partitions slide out from both ends of a sheetrock wall to produce a do-it-yourself guest bedroom and bath next to the master suite; there are no permanent encroachments on valuable living space. A panel lacquered in automotive paint bisects the shower area and its two-headed fixture, creating a guest bath.

FIVE MINUTE BATHROOM 1999

Our design for the Five Minute Bathroom, a domestic prototype commissioned by *Wallpaper* magazine, explores the affinities between the body, fashion, and architecture. The prefabricated, freestanding unit arrives ready to be installed in any generic living space and accommodates in assembly-line fashion all of the tasks necessary to face the day. The molded fiberglass shell integrates not only wet functions (washing, eliminating) but also related activities, such as sleeping and dressing.

The Five Minute Bathroom is composed of three basic elements—the water closet, the dressing closet, and the vanity, a digitally activated, Janus-faced mirror that serves back-to-back washing and dressing zones. The water closet organizes activities that involve water: a unisex urinal and toilet, "rain" shower activated by a foot pedal, and sink with smart mirror, which displays information (time, weight, and weather) and body close-ups. The dressing closet bridges wet zone (for storing cosmetics) and dry zone (for storing clothing). This walk-through wardrobe mirrors the form of the human body, categorizing items vertically: shampoo, hats, and helmets are at the top; footwear at the bottom.

The notion that surfaces that line interiors behave like garments that clothe bodies informs the design of the self-supporting structural shell. The contoured skin of the Five Minute Bathroom is similar in function to the makeup and lotions, underwear and outerwear it efficiently stores, a malleable surface that enables the performing body to fashion identity.

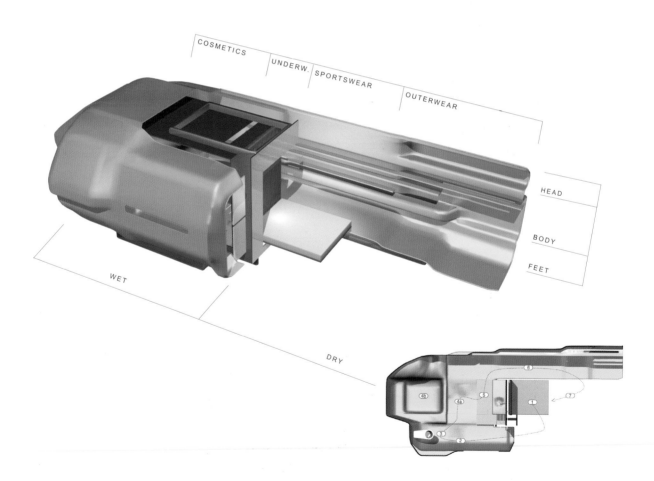

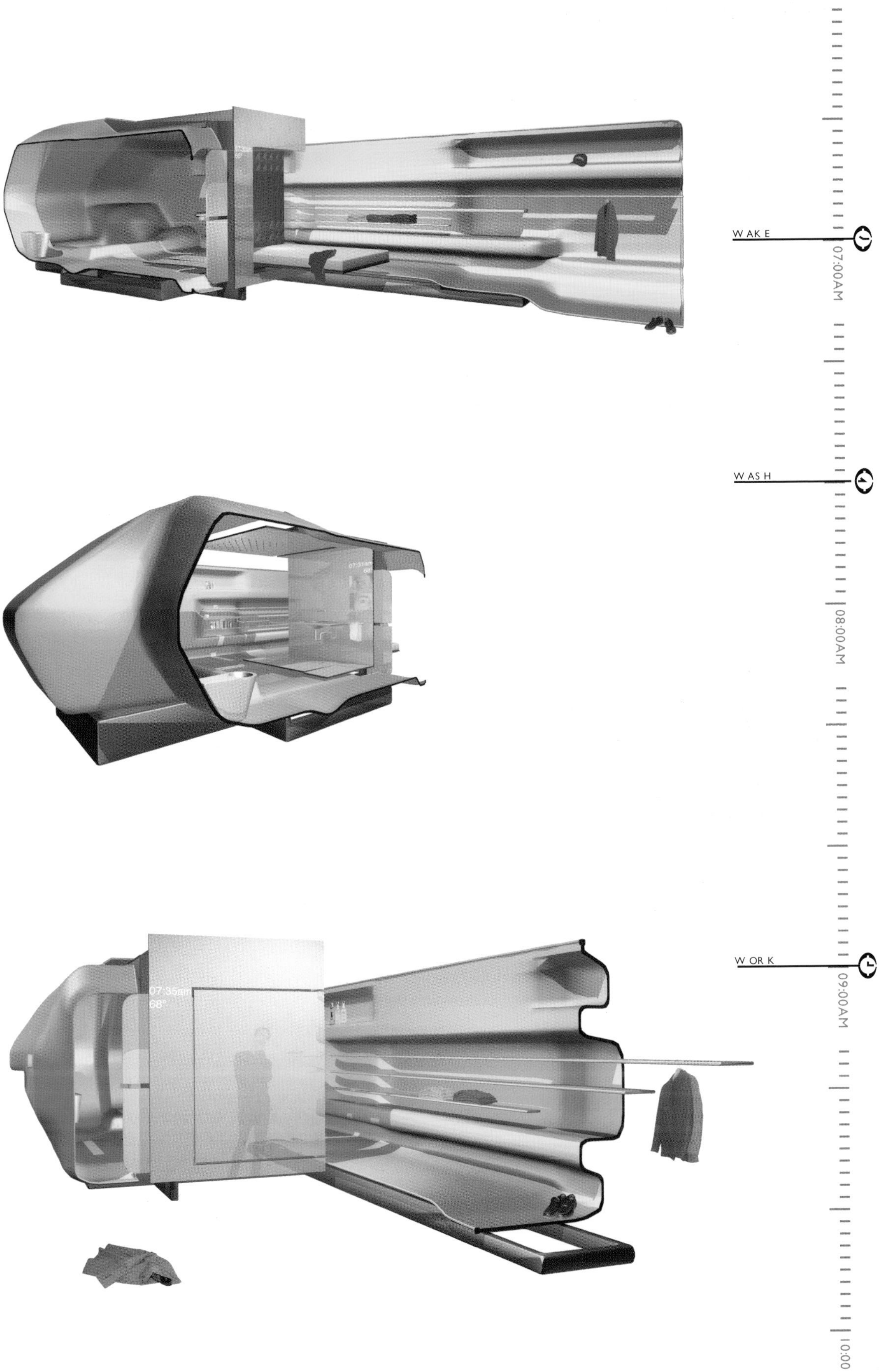

WAKE — 07:00AM

WASH

08:00AM

WORK — 09:00AM

10:00

SANDS LOFT NEW YORK, NEW YORK, 2000

Conventional notions of public and private space coupled with the requirement to accommodate guest rooms can compromise the very essence of loft living: the luxury of inhabiting an open space unencumbered by walls and partitions. The Sands loft follows a different path: it features a "leisure landscape," a dynamic freestanding element that organizes the space into a series of overlapping, front-to-back, multipurpose zones for dining, entertaining, bathing, and sleeping. Sliding translucent screens divide these areas only when privacy is desired. Our intervention—more a hybrid of furniture and architecture than a work that adheres to conventional distinctions between rigid enclosure and upholstered interior—integrates hard and soft, architecture and decoration.

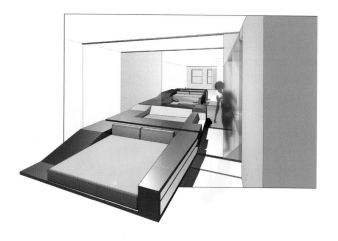

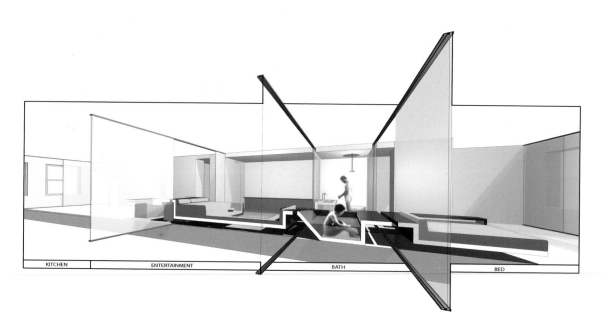

KITCHEN · ENTERTAINMENT · BATH · BED

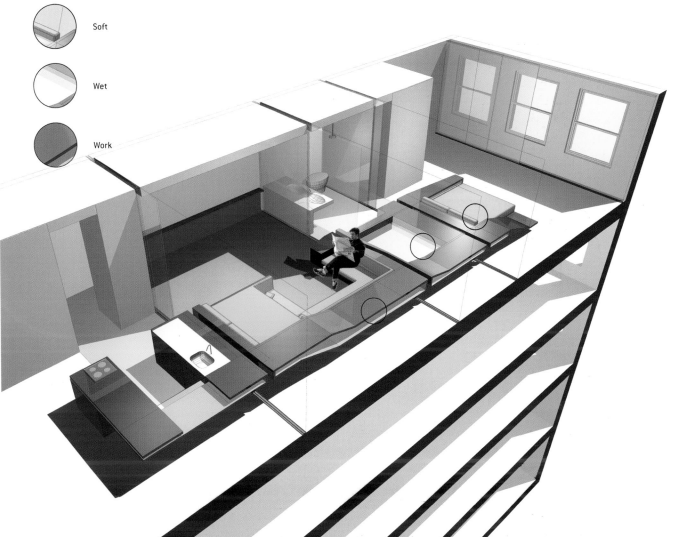

Soft

Wet

Work

THE FOUNDRY NEW YORK, NEW YORK, 2000–2001

Driven by the conviction that design-savvy consumers seek attractive alternatives to banal high-rise residential buildings, Manhattan developer Gotham Construction commissioned us to design the lobbies and public interiors of two new rental properties, the Foundry. The buildings are located in Hell's Kitchen, on the far west side of Manhattan, and are connected by a common courtyard.

For the larger of the lobbies, the client asked us to reconcile opposites: new and old, smooth and rough, organic and inorganic. Recalling nested Russian dolls, the design consists of two interlocking volumes. An inner shell constructed from smooth synthetic materials (painted sheetrock, terrazzo, hot rolled steel) appears to float within the building's brick enclosure; we lined this shell with textured surfaces associated with nature (green-tinted concrete encrusted with water-washed pebbles). Structural columns encased in fiberglass pierce backlit cutouts in the floor and ceiling of the inner shell, dematerializing the boundaries of the outer structure. The concierge desk and a perimeter bench, both made of molded terrazzo, emerge from the floor. Inset felt floor panels and Ultrasuede upholstery offer a softer counterpoint to the polished terrazzo.

The design of the somewhat smaller lobby of the adjoining building juxtaposes a similar palette of contrasting materials. A white terrazzo floor is suspended above walnut floorboards that fold vertically to create a dramatic backlit canted wall visible from the street. Designed to capture the attention of pedestrians, this receding plane visually connects city street with vestibule and elevator lobby within.

THE GYM: A SITE FOR SORE EYES

HVAC systems that make us either too hot or too cold; office chairs that induce back pain and carpal tunnel syndrome; poorly insulated walls that impair privacy by transmitting unwanted noise: usually, we become aware of our senses only through some flaw in the physical environment that makes us feel uncomfortable. Otherwise, architecture, considered a "visual art," participates in what critics have referred to as the "scopic regime of modernity," privileging vision, a "higher" sense affiliated with the intellect, and suppressing taste, smell, and touch, "lower" senses associated with the abject.[1]

1. There is a large body of literature devoted to exploring how Western culture valorizes vision and intellect at the expense of the biological body, including Michel Foucault, *Discipline and Punish* (New York: Vintage Books, 1979); Martin Jay, *Downcast Eyes: The Denigration of Vision in Twentieth-Century French Thought* (Berkeley and Los Angeles: University of California Press, 1993); and Jonathan Crary, *Techniques of the Observer* (Cambridge: MIT Press, 1990).

But the gym, a space dedicated to the cultivation of the body, is the rare building type with the potential to counteract this prevailing tendency. In these mirror-lined interiors, sweating bodies, wired to headphones and video monitors, assume a variety of poses that bring them into direct contact with all the surfaces of architecture—walls, floors, and even ceilings. Regretfully, most health clubs, driven by the forces of the marketplace, do not exploit the architectural potential of this largely unexamined building type. If these facilities, like the bodies they shelter, come in a variety of shapes, sizes, and colors (geared to a diverse audience of young and old, amateur and professional, straight and gay), they nonetheless generally adhere to a generic design formula. While the following observations are drawn from my own regular workouts, they also apply to a wide range of gyms that I have visited, all of which crowd members into banal interiors whose configurations promote social interactions that perpetuate rather than challenge problematic cultural notions about health, beauty, gender, and sexuality.[2] And yet, exceeding the narrow-minded

2. It goes almost without saying that gyms embody our culture's obsession with youth, beauty, and sex. In these Foucauldian theaters of discipline and surveillance, men and women subject themselves to grueling workout routines in an attempt to shore up their vulnerable self-images. Problematic cultural notions of bodily perfection reproduce deep-seated cultural anxieties about masculinity and femininity.

vision of their owners, these ordinary spaces can and do operate in exceptional way, sometimes subverting rather than confirming social norms. Wedding the ideals of machine-age modernism to the promise of digital technologies, health clubs possess the rare capacity to engage all the senses as exercising bodies traffic between actual and virtual space.

Franco Albini's "Apartment for a Single Man," equipped with barbells and Le Corbusier's architectural renderings of domestic dwellings inhabited by burly boxers sparring with punching bags, exemplifies how gym culture incorporates two linked trademarks of modern architecture: an unabashed promotion of the Spartan values of health and hygiene and an obsession with machines and equipment. In fact, gym design evokes that iconic modernist space: the factory. Ostensibly functionally determined spaces for the production of hard bodies, gyms are typically open, unadorned spaces clad in durable materials (rubber, metals, mirrors) and filled with exercise equipment laid out in assembly-line fashion. Following the logic of the workout routine, this layout is configured to allow members to move efficiently from one exercise machine, tailored to isolate and to develop a particular muscle—biceps, quadriceps, deltoids, hamstrings—to the next.

Surely, Le Corbusier and Charlotte Perriand would have admired Cybex equipment, which takes one step further the signature chrome metal frame they employed in chairs like the *fauteuil à dossier basculant* and the *grand confort*. Here a white-painted metal structure supports not only upholstered surfaces that come into contact with the body but moving weight stacks. Black cables and pulleys link muscles with weights, reflecting both modernism's general fetishization of the mechanical and also its particular conflation of body, building, and machine. As humans occupy the machine's metallic framework, the biological and the manufactured become one, joined in a synchronized dance of mechanical movement that recalls Oskar Schlemmer's "Mechanical Ballet."

But if form follows workout, contrary to expectation, gym planning generally betrays the promised integration of body and equipment. Ideally, the layout of these secular temples to the body should mirror the human figure, a concept that, strangely enough, evokes Renaissance architectural drawings—from Francesco Di Giorgio to Leonardo—that superimposed nude male figures over church floor plans. Machines that work adjacent muscles should, optimally, be next to one another, beginning with the neck at one end and working down to the feet at the other—a configuration that would facilitate a full-body workout, a routine that conceives of the body as a holistic entity composed of interrelated, contiguous muscular movements. But instead, most gyms are configured to facilitate the split routine adopted not by athletes but by bodybuilders who, like Jim Weider and Arnold Schwarzenegger, favor dividing the body into isolated groups (chest, arms, legs, back, and abdominals), muscle groups that can be mixed and matched during independent training sessions. Spatially, the split routine groups equipment dedicated to related body parts in independent clusters. From the viewpoint of efficient space planning, this divide-and-conquer strategy lends itself to shoehorning equipment into tight, often irregularly shaped floor plans. At the same time, it mirrors and perpetuates contemporary culture's fetishization of body parts. From print ads to television, media bombards us with cropped images of women, and increasingly men, rendered in fragments.[3]

3. For a discussion of the psychoanalytic implications of the print media's rendering of fragmented images of the female body, see Diana Fuss, "Fashion and the Homospectatorial Look," *Critical Inquiry* 18:4 (Summer 1992): 713–37.

As gym design isolates body parts, it isolates the sexes as well. While specialty facilities like Lucille Roberts feature pink-painted equipment earmarked for a specifically female clientele, health clubs are for the most part coed. And yet, despite the unisex design of the gym, gender segregation plays a subtle but nevertheless significant role. Male and female members alike tend to gravitate to equipment that works those choice parts of the anatomy accentuated by popular culture: dividing the body at the waist, men develop chest, back, and arms, while women concentrate on thighs, legs, and buttocks. If many women steer clear of upper-body workouts for fear of looking "manly," men avoid machines that place them in "womanly" postures. The hip abduction requires wide-spread thighs, while the "butt blaster" puts users on hands and knees, passive postures that call attention to the most vulnerable part of the male anatomy—the crotch and anus—immediately conjuring the phobic specter of femininity and homosexuality.

Areas reserved exclusively for free weights and fitness classrooms reinforce this separation of the sexes as effectively as the doors that divide male and female locker rooms. Many women find weight training in general, and free weights in particular, an alienating male precinct; this is why some gyms cordon off "girls only" weight sections. Other women gravitate to the glass-walled refuge of fitness classrooms. But if large numbers of women, enjoying the supportive encouragement of groups, enroll in classes, men, considering instruction feminizing, tend to prefer solo activities like weight training.

But free weights also separate the men from the boys. By most accounts, free weights are no more effective at building the upper body than machines, but they nonetheless possess the mystique of the professional bodybuilder. If slickly designed Cybex machines are akin to designer suits, then free weights invoke worn dungarees and are considered more authentic, more difficult, and hence more manly than their mechanical counterparts. Ironically, the free-weight area, a stage for the performance of primitive virility, reverses traditional gender codes, presenting men as objects, not only of their own subjective scrutiny but of the gaze of others as well. Contrary to

Cybex's concealing thicket of metallic moving parts, weight racks maintain an unobstructed horizon line that, by never violating bench-press eye height, ensures maximum visibility from all corners of the gym. Further calling attention to themselves with grunts and groans, bodybuilders and their spotting partners willingly display themselves in intimate interlocking postures, with reclining eyes directed upward to standing genitals.

In Duchampian fashion, both free weights and exercise machines obey a contradictory logic. These precisely calibrated instruments function to build useless muscles, developed primarily to be admired. But if the incentive behind weight training is cosmetic, some argue that aerobics, by boosting our cardiovascular systems, improves both health and self-image. Yet while few challenge the utility of aerobic machines, when evaluated from a functionalist design perspective, they too are illogical devices that compensate for our sedentary daily lives by providing indoor, condensed versions of outdoor sports like jogging (treadmill), boating (rowing machine), biking (Lifecycle), and cross-country skiing (NordicTrack)—all activities that most of us do not have the time, skill, or space to enjoy. Strangely enough, even a chore like climbing stairs is simulated at the gym, perhaps appealing to an apartment dweller's inner yearning for domestic life in a multistory dwelling.

Enhancing the simulation effect of the gym, computerized keyboards attached to aerobic machines spatialize energy expenditure by mimicking actual topographies. For example, after the user grips poles attached to sliding skis, the Body Trek cross-trainer offers the following program options: "walk in the park," "Himalayan trek," "Vail pass." Equating calorie burning with transport, aerobic machines inspire us to work harder as they attempt to overcome the monotony of the exerciser's actual location in interior space. Interestingly enough, aerobic equipment actually reverses the logic of the vehicles (bikes, boats, stairs) it emulates.

Expending energy, once a means to fuel devices invented to quickly convey us through different kinds of geographical spaces, becomes, within the static confines of the gym, an end in itself.

Spaces rife with cultural contradictions, health clubs literally capitalize on contemporary culture's ambivalent obsession with the sensuous body, a body forever subject to temptation and excess; its unruly appetites must be curbed, disciplined, and controlled. Paradoxically, having internalized society's discomfort with the carnal and the abject, we dedicate precious leisure hours in a closely monitored interior space to "work out." In the locker room, we remove our street clothes, ostensibly divesting ourselves of outward indicators of occupation and social status. Clad only in uniform T-shirt, shorts, and sneakers, we enter the gym floor, a social space where hierarchies are defined not so much by class and wealth as by the status conferred by being in good shape. Here we harness energy, motivated by the often unachievable goal of making over our recalcitrant flesh into a facsimile of the ephemeral airbrushed images of perfect bodies disseminated by the media. We congratulate ourselves for visiting the gym on a regular basis, a physical ritual that represents the triumph of will over appetite, mind over matter.

But self-discipline ultimately gives way to sensation. "Achieving failure," completing a set of repetitions to the point of muscle exhaustion, inevitably requires us to concentrate on our contracting limbs at work. The very process of triumphing over the body forces encounters, sometimes painful, with our physical selves, a dimension of our beings that we middle- and upper-class folk typically ignore in our daily lives, which are consumed by pursuits that require intellectual, not physical labor.

And by putting us in touch with our bodies, the gym heightens our awareness of the built environment. Requiring the user to lie prone with eyes turned upward, certain exercises, including bench presses and sit-ups, activate a surface of buildings that as upright beings we too often ignore—the ceiling. Some positions, like those for the prone leg curl, butt blaster, and ab crunch, direct our attention to the floor. But an exercise like stretching puts us directly into tactile contact with all of the horizontal and vertical surfaces of architecture—which we often look at but rarely touch—inviting us to press our bodies against resilient mats and vinyl wall coverings. Even less acrobatic exercises, like bicep and tricep curls, require us to consider how familiar postures like standing and sitting implicate gravity and space.

In the process of soliciting haptic responses, gyms reorganize vision as well, inviting us to see both others and ourselves in new and often startling ways. Health clubs differ from conventional, inwardly directed interiors where pieces of furniture are arranged facing each other to promote social interaction. Instead, gyms typically solve the problem of organizing a variety of solitary activities by orienting equipment in rows that face a mirror-lined periphery, inviting us to scrutinize our virtual reflections as we toil. Considered from a cosmetic viewpoint, mirrors make many gyms, often located in basements, appear brighter and less claustrophobic. From the vantage of trainers, they facilitate self-monitoring, enabling beginners to visually ensure correct form and posture. Counteracting the fragmenting logic of exercise machines, which isolate body parts, mirrors integrate. By reinstating the visual perception of the entire body, mirrors initiate a dynamic interplay between seeing and feeling, visual integration and physical fragmentation. For example, seated at the chest-press machine, my attention shifts between experiencing my pecs at work and regarding my entire body in the glass. This experience recalls early childhood, when infants, during the awkward phase of learning to coordinate their motor movements, first catch sight of their own reflections. But contrary to a

Lacanian, who might argue that this replaying of the mirror stage is alienating, in the context of the gym it proves exhilarating, offering the rare opportunity to reconcile eye, mind, and body.

Mirrors promote voyeurism as well as narcissism, affording the opportunity to check out other scantily clad physiques. As I stand facing the mirror and confront my own image, the mirror's reflective depth allows me to surreptitiously survey individuals to my right, to my left, and behind me. With only a slight rotation of my head, I can, unnoticed, absorb the full panoramic spectacle or, alternatively, zoom in on a particularly captivating fellow gym member. Not really a form of camouflage, the mirror functions more like an open closet. Most gym-goers are well versed in the techniques of mirror surveillance, an unspoken but nevertheless widespread code of visual conduct. Bolder gym members employ this reflective surface as a tool of seduction and engage in scopic games of cat and mouse, shamelessly exchanging furtive glances with strangers.

Mirrors, by allowing spectators to shuttle back and forth between narcissism and voyeurism as they exercise, sanction actions considered taboo in most social contexts. But this fluctuation between embodied self-awareness and virtual space is reflected by another increasingly prominent component of health-club design—digital technologies. The flicker of televisual images viewed from screens suspended from the ceiling and attached to the brightly lit instrumentation panels of aerobic machines now competes with the seductive pleasure of watching reflected bodies. Like mirrors, these transparent surfaces also resemble windows that frame virtual views to alternative worlds.

The awkward attachment of electronic keyboards to aerobic machines underscores how they, like the health clubs in which they are used, uncomfortably straddle two eras and ideologies—the machine age and the digital age. Initially, the introduction of these blinking control systems to the handlebars of Stair Masters and Lifecycles seemed to enhance the functional logic of devices invented to elevate heart rate by offering users a range of data—floors climbed, distance traveled, steps per minute, power output, total calories expended—that precisely chart physical activity over time. While we bemoan our fast-paced culture, we nevertheless consent to spend spare hours in a space entirely governed by time-keeping devices displayed not only from walls but from within the slick surfaces of aerobic equipment.

These flashing instrumentation panels, more sci-fi than high tech, reveal how, increasingly, health clubs are modeling themselves after Hollywood rather than Cape Kennedy. In contrast to equipment invented to discipline the biological body in actual space, media (print and electronic) transports gym members into virtual space. Only a short time ago, gym-goers could exercise the option of sporting portable Walkmans or leaning sweat-stained newspapers and magazines precariously against stationary bikes, cerebral diversions from the spectacle of half-clothed bodies reflected in mirrors. But more recently, increasingly sophisticated built-in multimedia technologies, which integrate sight and sound, allow exercisers alternative virtual escape routes while they work out. Complementing the collective activity of watching closed-captioned television, members can also plug into multimedia systems like E-zone that, wired into each machine, allow users to select television and compact-disc programs to suit their mood. A new generation of Lifecycles now allows members to surf the Internet as they peddle.

As the hum of headphones mixes with the din of clanging metal plates, and the glow of television and video screens competes with stolen glimpses of reflected bodies, the increasing incorporation of media within gyms makes even more unstable the already tenuous boundaries between virtual and physical space and further heightens the thrilling experience of negotiating between the realms of mind and body. On the verge of sensory overload, gym culture now finds itself at a critical crossroads. Multimedia technologies threaten to tip this delicate balance in favor of spectacle. The adage "no pain, no gain" has been replaced by "exertainment." Virtual space distracts, effectively diverting exercisers from the pain and drudgery of the workout routine by eradicating body self-consciousness. Blinded by the light of digital displays, we are in danger of losing touch with our own bodies as we strive to model ourselves after the ideal bodies projected from strategically placed monitors.

Rather than give in to this popular trend, if patrons and their architects were to treat health-club design with the same seriousness as they do more dignified institutional commissions like museums and libraries, gym facilities might meet their potential as unique social spaces with the capacity to engage all of the body's senses. Why should we settle for the present crop of formulaic interiors clad in monotonous floor coverings and cheap acoustical tiles and filled with row upon row of isolated equipment? Combining the best aspects of mechanical and electronic technologies, gyms hold the promise of becoming truly hybrid spaces that can erase traditional distinctions between hardware and software, spatially integrating the human body with architecture, machines, and electronics. Imagine jogging on a "built-in" treadmill embedded in the actual floor surface that inclines and declines in response to an interactive digital program that simulates different terrain. Or stretching in a space with resilient undulating floors and walls that conform to the contours of your moving body as you watch programs projected directly from floor-to-ceiling mirrors. The future holds these and many other opportunities for designers: gyms might offer a whole range of experiences that could invite exercising bodies to explore the dematerialized edges of virtual space as they physically engage the sensuous surfaces of the built environment.

ADAPTED FROM *ACHIEVING FAILURE: GYM CULTURE,* ED. BILL ARNING (NEW YORK: THREAD WAXING SPACE, 2000).

ACCESS HOUSE ST. SIMONS ISLAND, GEORGIA, 2001–2002

The Access House, a beach house on an island off the coast of Georgia, reconsiders a ubiquitous feature of the American vacation home: the picture window. A continuous floor slab spirals vertically, creating interconnected multi-purpose living levels, each with spectacular ocean vistas framed through floor-to-ceiling glass. But if these window walls afford panoramic views, they also might engender a sense of vulnerability. Particularly at night, the insubstantial glass boundary can provoke feelings of defenselessness, leading the occupants to fear that they and their property are susceptible to voyeurism, burglary, and even physical harm.

The Access House solves the dilemmas posed by the picture window with the E:core, a high-tech take on the American hearth that functions as both the spatial and the visual heart of the home. Monitors embedded in the E:core display television, video, and the Internet as well as closed-circuit images transmitted from surveillance cameras placed throughout the house. These multiple electronic windows complement actual views of the landscape and also function as a benevolent Big Brother that safeguards the house and its occupants.

Yet the Access House never loses sight of the tactile body. The E:core contains within its branchlike form building systems that ensure physical and sensual well-being: HVAC, bathroom fixtures, and kitchen appliances. In lieu of furniture, the E:core incorporates upholstered membranes on surfaces that touch the human skin, encouraging exchanges between ocular and haptic perception.

SITE PLAN

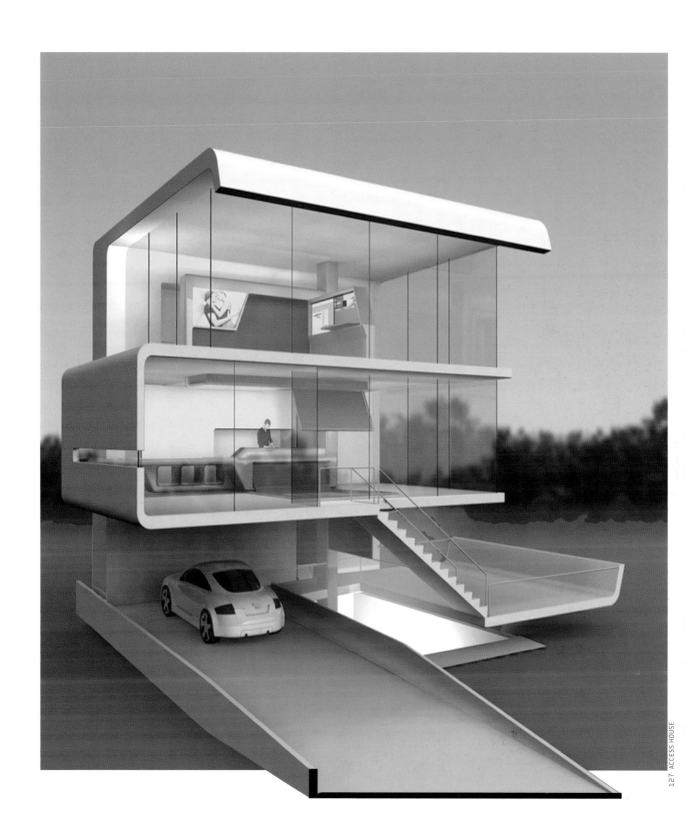

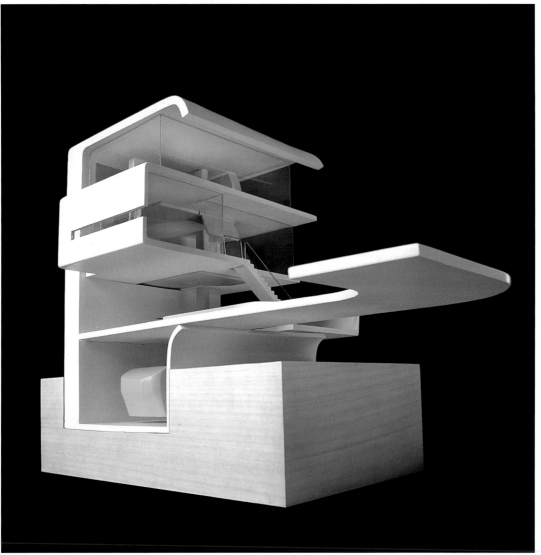

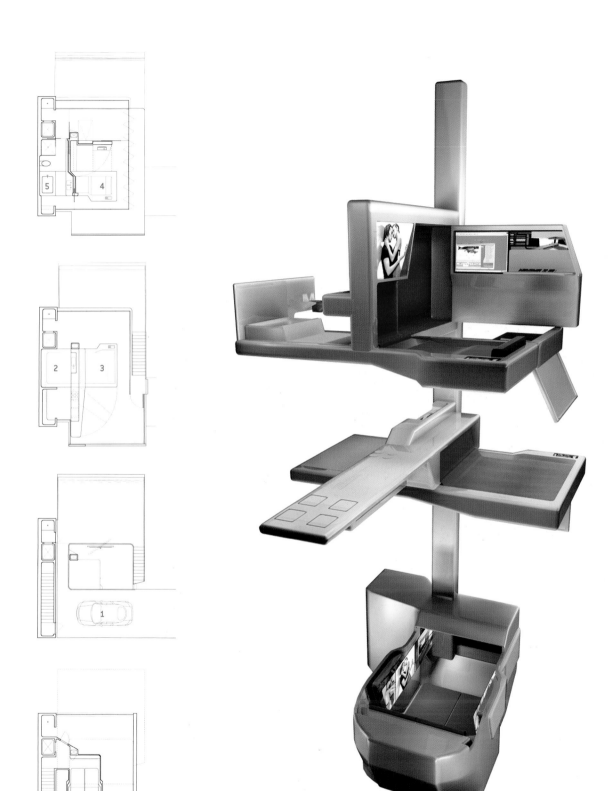

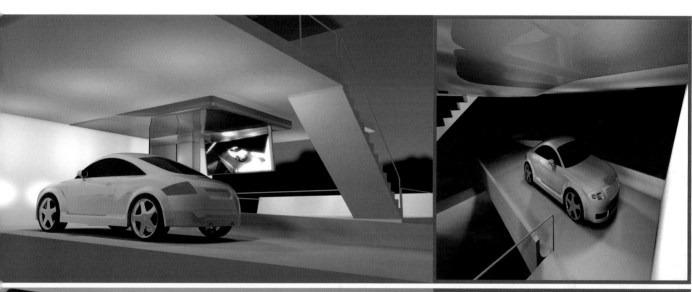

1
Park
A monitor greets guests arriving by car; the drawbridge stair descends, inviting them to the main living level.

2
Lounge
On the second level, the owners and their guests can relax on a couch embedded within the heated floor slab, a cozy vantage point from which to watch closed-circuit images, videos, or actual waves breaking on the beach.

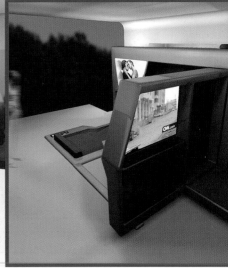

3
Cook
The kitchen island functions as the central command station for the house: outfitted with control panels and resembling an automobile dashboard, it regulates dumbwaiter, appliances, HVAC, and media equipment.

4
Sleep
A pivoting partition swings out from the storage wall between bedroom and master bath, revealing on one side a home office and on the other a fold-down guest bed.

5
Cleanse
Digital displays integrated into the bathroom vanity juxtapose media images with personal reflections.

6
Retreat
Nestled inside the subterranean womb, the homeowners can recline on bucket seats and watch images (closed-circuit or live-media) displayed on a strip of plasma screens.

In our design for the Millennium residence, the renovation of a two-thousand-square-foot apartment a stone's throw from Lincoln Center, we first decided to raze the existing walls, which divided the space into a series of isolated rooms, in order to develop a flexible open plan suited to the client's brief, which requested a resilient dance floor for ballet practice, accommodations for out-of-town guests, and plenty of storage space.

The domestic programs (entry, living-dining, dance practice, study, master bedroom, and master bath) form a chain of overlapping spaces that flow around the centerpiece of the project—a service core incorporating plumbing (master and guest bath) and storage (master closet, home entertainment, bookshelves, appliances). Unlike the typical core, which is treated as a solid, opaque mass that shields its contents from view, our design selectively reveals. The core, made of acid-etched glass, is also the apartment's principal light source, or lantern. Backlit bodies and household objects are silhouetted against this glowing container.

By inverting traditional notions of domestic decorum, of what is deemed acceptable to behold, the Millennium residence sponsors a diverse range of activities within the limited square footage of a New York City high-rise apartment.

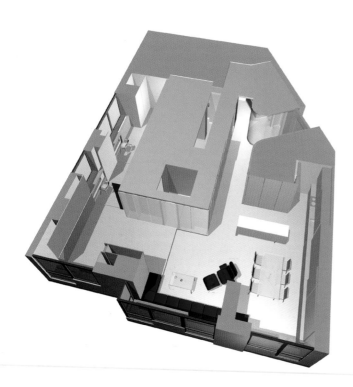

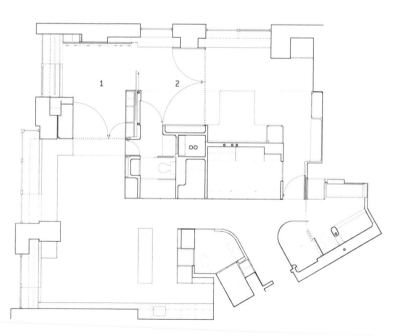

1

Dance Studio/Guest 1

In the dance practice area, a wall panel pivots to reveal a Murphy bed, converting the space into a private guest suite with bath.

2
Study/Guest 2
A pocket door and a pair of pivoting wall panels separate a private study or second guest room from the master brdroom. The subdivided space is equipped with its own entry to the shared guest bath.

960 FOOD HARTFORD, CONNECTICUT, 2002–2003

Ergotectonic principles governed our design for 960 Food, a restaurant located in G. Fox, an Art Deco department store recently converted into a mixed-use commercial retail complex for downtown Hartford. Located within the building's street-level retail arcade, the project features a palette of "performative" materials, each earmarked to sustain a different activity: durable poured-epoxy floors and epoxy-painted walls withstand mall traffic, stainless-steel counters provide easy-to-clean surfaces for food preparation, and soft materials (carpeting and upholstery) comfortably accommodate seated diners.

The dramatic two-story space integrates two related programs: food court concessions on the first level and a dining balcony/bar above. From the exterior, the metal-and-glass storefront showcases customers as they ascend a red carpeted staircase. Inside, a striking folded sheetrock plane signals the upstairs dining area, defines a café on the first level, and forms a suspended canopy that hugs the underside of the unfinished concrete ceiling above.

A double-duty linear counter—communal lunch table by day and bar by night—commands the dining balcony. Simply by modulating lighting levels, the client can change the mood of the space, shifting from a brightly lit food court catering to office workers and college students to a dimly lit cocktail lounge catering to patrons of nearby Hartford Stage.

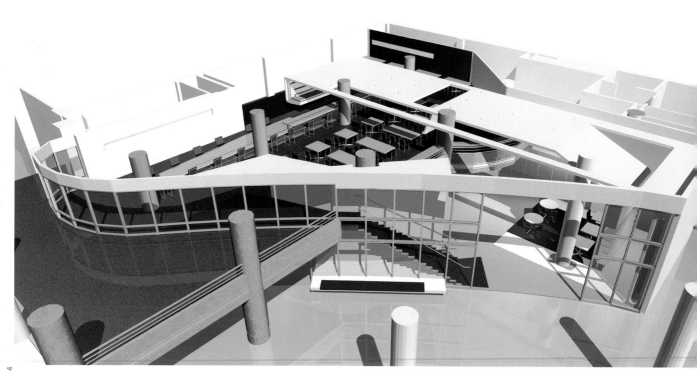

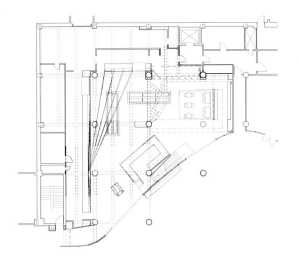

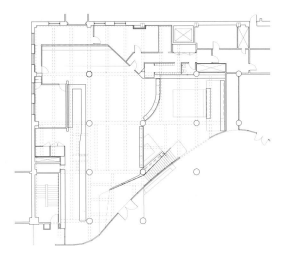

24/7 BUSINESS HOTEL COOPER-HEWITT, NATIONAL DESIGN MUSEUM, NEW YORK, NEW YORK, 2002–2003

Our design for the 24/7 Business Hotel, commissioned by the Cooper-Hewitt for the exhibition "New Hotels for Global Nomads," takes advantage of the porous boundaries between work and leisure. We reconfigured the standard hotel layout of twelve-by-twenty-four-foot rooms arranged in pairs with back-to-back wet cores. Instead, our prefabricated modular unit integrates furniture and enclosure within a volume made of two principal materials: a molded, waterproof fiberglass shell and a pliable lining, used for flooring and upholstery. Privacy screens that double as projection screens, operated by remote control, descend from tracks embedded in the ceiling, subdividing the space when seclusion is required. Storage, from window to corridor, is integrated into the folded membrane. Conceived of as a miniature spa, the bathroom contains a single basin that merges sink, shower, and bath; the pool can be enjoyed alone, with a partner, or with business associates.

No longer reserved for circulation alone, the hotel corridor is bordered by a banquette that encourages conversation. Each hotel room has a retractable facade; with this element in the open position, the rooms can merge with this vital social connector, creating a dynamic semipublic lounge overlooking the hotel's top-lit central atrium. Collapsing traditional distinctions between building scale and human scale, between stable shell and freestanding furniture, the 24/7 Business Hotel offers a multitasking environment literally molded to fit the personal and professional needs of the global business traveler.

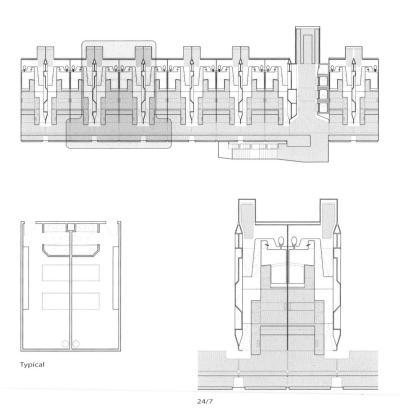

Typical

24/7

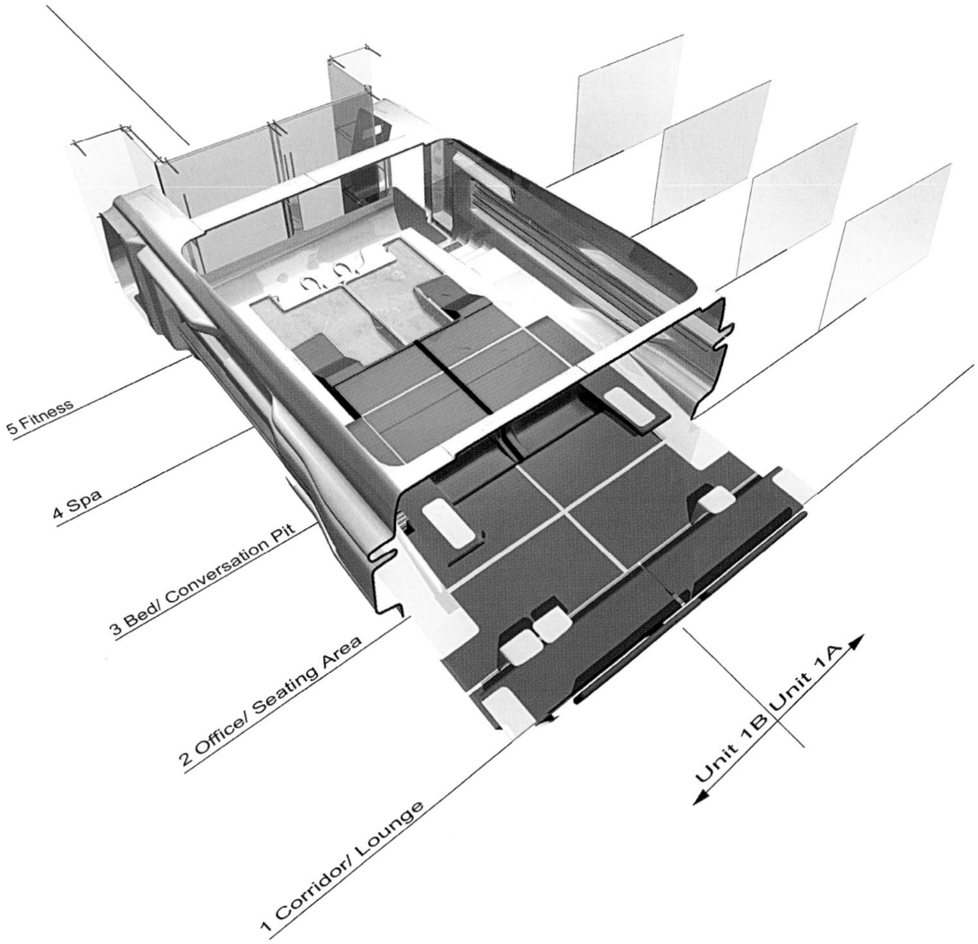

5 Fitness

4 Spa

3 Bed/ Conversation Pit

2 Office/ Seating Area

1 Corridor/ Lounge

Unit 1B Unit 1A

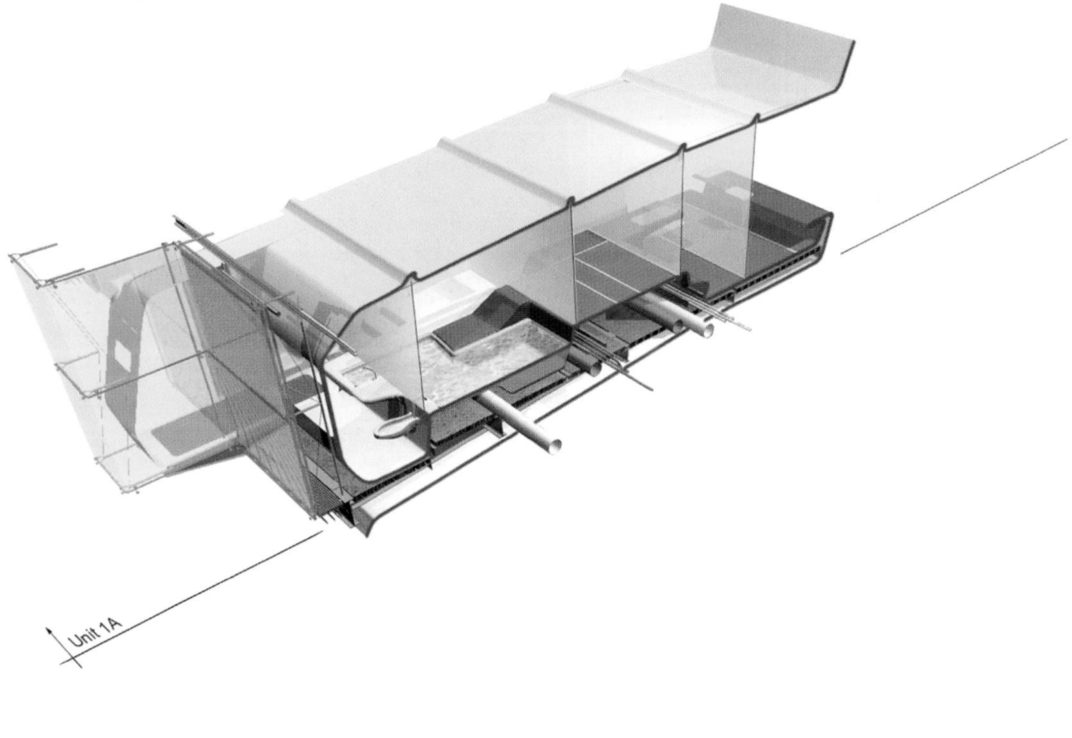

Unit 1A

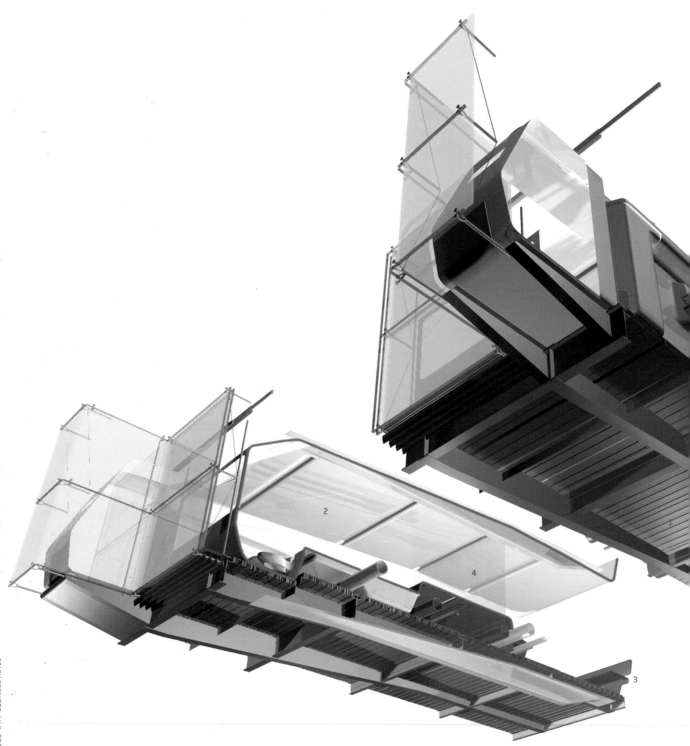

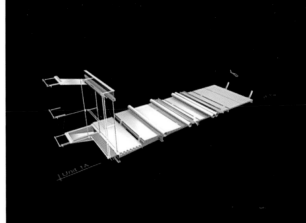

1
Infrastructure

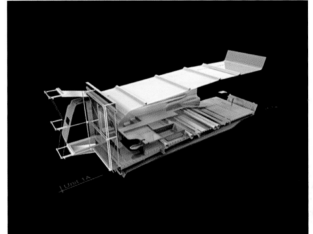

2
Shell

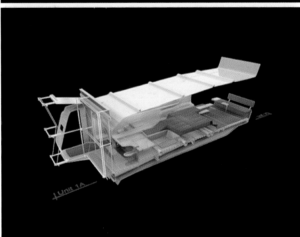

3
Soft

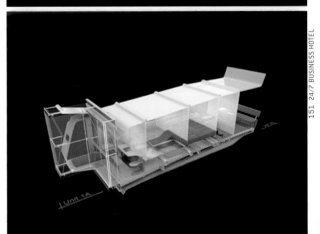

4
Privacy/Projection
Screens

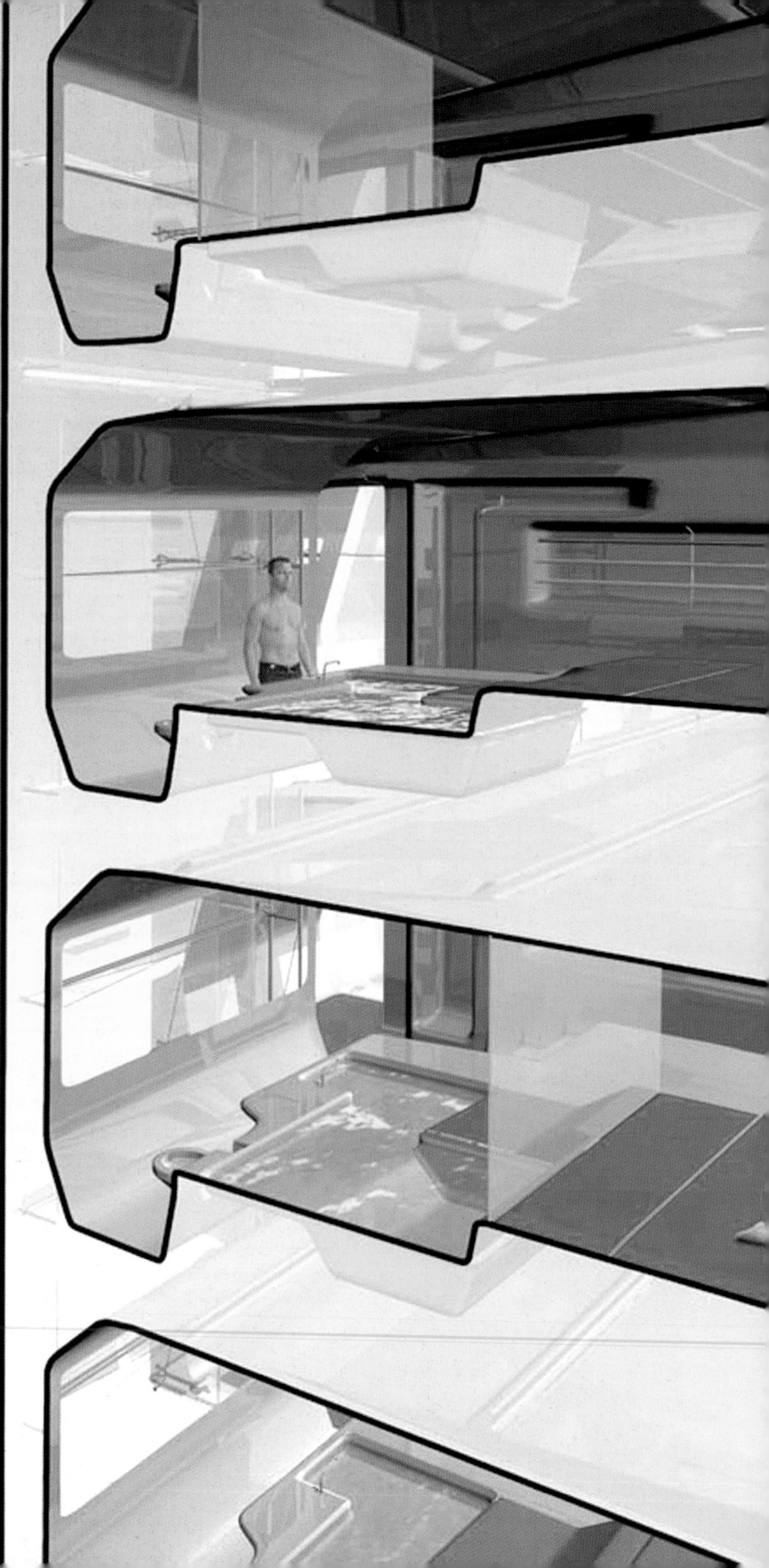

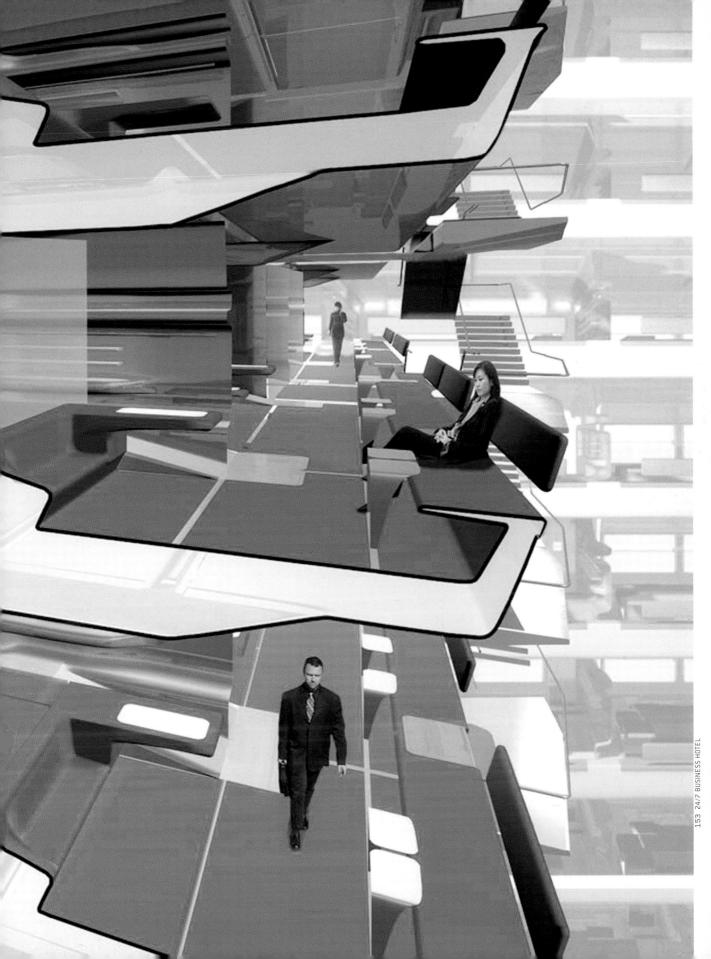

153 24/7 BUSINESS HOTEL

🕐 **7:15 AM**
Wake

🕐 **9:00 AM**
Work

🕐 **5:00 PM**
Work out

🕐 **9:30 PM**
Relax

OLYMPIC TRAINERS "EPHEMERAL STRUCTURES IN THE CITY OF ATHENS" COMPETITION, 2002–2003

One of the many new projects associated with the Athens 2004 Olympic Games was a competition for an easily assembled, demountable structure for the streets of the city. Our proposal, Olympic Trainers, harks back to ancient Greek culture, where in cities like Olympia—the site of the first Olympic Games—gyms (*palestrae*) were located in the very heart of the urban tissue.

Olympic Trainers promotes fitness by encouraging people of all ages and nationalities to become active participants rather than passive spectators. Within a series of pavilions made of mix-and-match prefabricated PVC panels, which can be assembled in different sizes according to the configuration of a specific site, visitors become amateur athletes training for events represented in the Olympics—swimming, running, rowing, and cycling. As visitors work out on machines, they are reminded that the aerobic activities we habitually perform inside gyms and health clubs have a counterpart in outdoor sports.

Human energy expended inside is registered by images projected outside: calories are converted into electricity that powers a series of projectors; these projectors in turn transmit virtual moving images of Olympic athletes onto a glass screen that divides interior from exterior, trainers from pedestrians. Inside, these images inspire the exercisers: the harder visitors work, the more legible the projection becomes. Outside, this spectacle of bodies, both taped and live, commands the attention of pedestrians.

Olympic Trainers registers the tactile as well as the visual. Sweating bodies, wired to headphones and video monitors, assume various postures that bring them into direct contact with the cushioned shell. Olympic Trainers engages all of the senses as exercisers traffic between actual and virtual space.

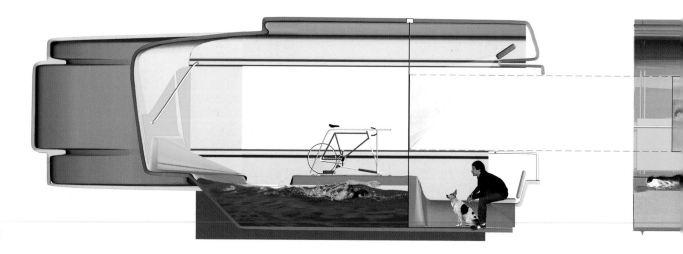

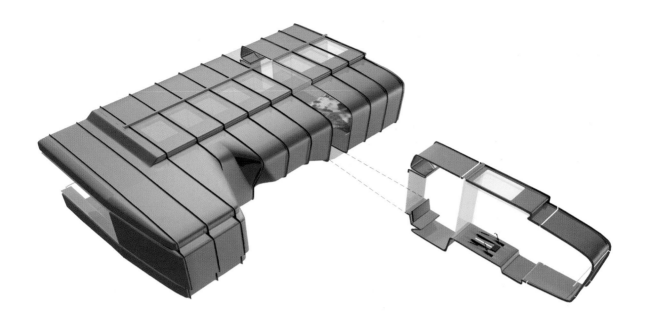

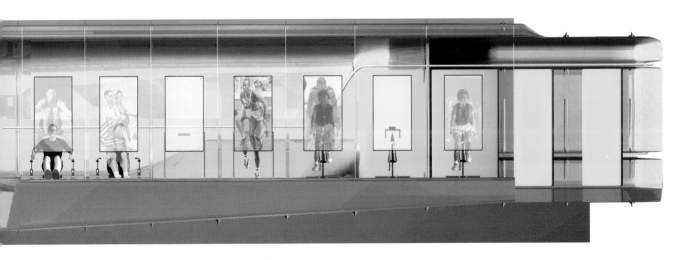

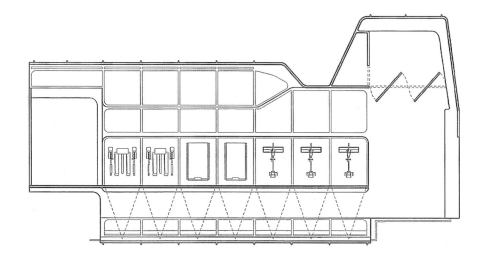

EASYHOTEL 2003

A project that builds on ideas we first explored in the 24/7 Business Hotel, easyHotel is a prefabricated modular hotel room commissioned by Stelios, a European entrepreneur known for his no-frills travel businesses, including easyJet and easyCar. Stelios discovered that cutting housekeeping costs would lower overhead and, as a consequence, room rates. The easyHotel concept: on-line booking, sheets and towels provided by vending machines, rebates for guests who clean their rooms. We capitalized on state-of-the-art digital fabrication techniques to devise a space-saving, easy-to-maintain hotel-room prototype, one that can be installed in retrofitted properties as well as new buildings.

Unlike a conventional hotel room—an enclosure with freestanding furniture and fixtures—easyHotel efficiently incorporates all domestic activities within a hospitality wall that also consolidates infrastructure (plumbing, lighting, electrical, and HVAC). Each prefabricated mix-and-match modular panel is assigned a specific use—shower, toilet, sink, bed—and may be assembled as either a single or a double.

Installation is remarkably easy: an adjustable "flex-strip" allows the length and width of each room to be modified according to the dimensions of a given building or site. Our design combines prefabricated components with standard materials (stud wall and sheetrock) and construction techniques, allowing for efficient on-site assembly. If it is used as part of a retrofit, the system is not constrained by exterior window configurations. The end wall of each unit includes a translucent window panel that, when erected behind an existing facade, allows the transmission of borrowed natural light.

High-performance materials are integral to fulfilling the goals of easyHotel. Waterproof fiberglass painted the company's signature orange is used in wet and high-traffic areas, where guests come into direct physical contact with the wall and floor. Soft surfaces—mattress and cushions—are wrapped in durable vinyl. The entire room can be wiped clean with only a damp cloth.

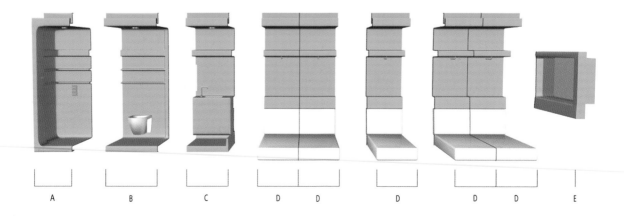

A   B   C   D   D   D   D   D   E

A
B
C
D
D
D
D
D

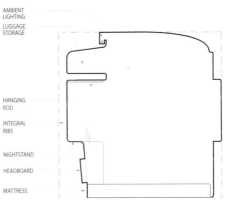

AMBIENT
LIGHTING

LUGGAGE
STORAGE

HANGING
ROD

INTEGRAL
RIBS

NIGHTSTAND

HEADBOARD

MATTRESS

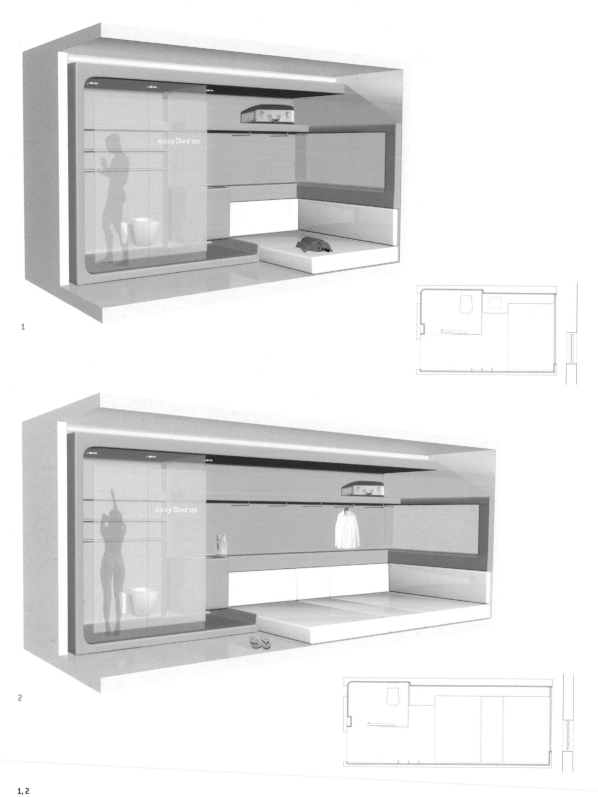

1

2

1, 2
Kit-of-Parts
Modular panels can be assembled to form two principal room types, a single and a double, as well as customized rooms: a double without bath, a single with two sinks, and so on.

CHARLES WORTHINGTON NEW YORK NEW YORK, NEW YORK, 2002–2003

Charles Worthington New York, the Manhattan flagship of a London-based cosmetics company, accommodates a varied program of salon, lounge, and offices. Our design brings together two qualities often associated with Soho lofts: the cool elegance of a gallery and the comfort of a residential loft.

After passing through oversized glass entry doors, visitors encounter a bent plane that defines a freestanding enclosure, a room within a room that appears to float within the refurbished nineteenth-century shell. This surface, painted Worthington's signature color, stone, forms the backdrop of the reception area and folds horizontally to create both an inset epoxy floor and a suspended ceiling. The folded sheetrock plane also creates a service pocket that conceals mechanical and lighting in the ceiling as well as back-of-house functions.

Backlit suspended soffits and underlit white-lacquer furniture dematerialize boundaries. Dramatic glass vases, also lit from below, rise from a cantilevered reception desk. An L-shaped sofa, suspended from a central structural column, creates an inviting lounge where clients can relax and chat as they enjoy the dynamic urban view.

In contrast to the arrangement at typical salons, where customers sit rigidly in assembly-line rows facing mirrored walls, Worthington features custom-designed movable styling stations that can be configured in various ways, either as freestanding elements or as pieces docked into a central storage platform. These units, together with the movable modular ottomans, allow for multiple spatial configurations that permit different activities to take place at different times—salon by day, event space at night.

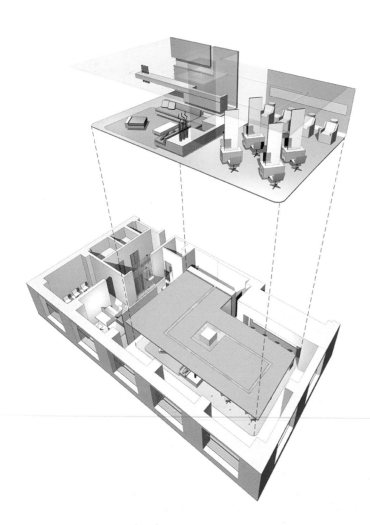

The theme of textiles informed our entry to an invited competition for a new interdepartmental classroom building at the Fashion Institute of Technology. Woven or knitted, textiles link the diverse disciplines and departments that make up FIT, from fashion (fabric) to painting (canvas). Hence, we conceived of the building as a well-dressed person clad in an ensemble of materials—woven glass on the exterior and gold carpeting and upholstery on the interior—as a strategy to weave together a series of interactive spaces for the FIT community.

Our project reinterprets the existing campus design vocabulary, which is characterized by buildings with two-story bases and slabs above. Two elements, a bar floating over a two-story plinth, form an inviting campus gateway that establishes a spatial and symbolic focus on West Twenty-eighth Street.

A golden "thread" begins at the entrance and defines a continuous circulation path through the building, from the soaring street-level atrium to the administrative roof terrace. Activated along its length by multipurpose student activity zones, this thread also bridges our project with the C Building, an existing 1950s campus mid-rise.

The project is fully sustainable, featuring natural ventilation, day-lighting, and green roofs, all aimed at improving quality of life while increasing energy efficiency. Like a raincoat, the building's unique textile cladding creates a breathable membrane that shields the building and its occupants from the elements (rain, sun, wind) while permitting it to draw energy and air directly from the outside environment.

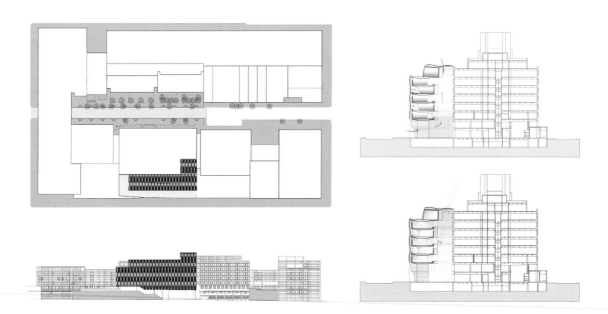

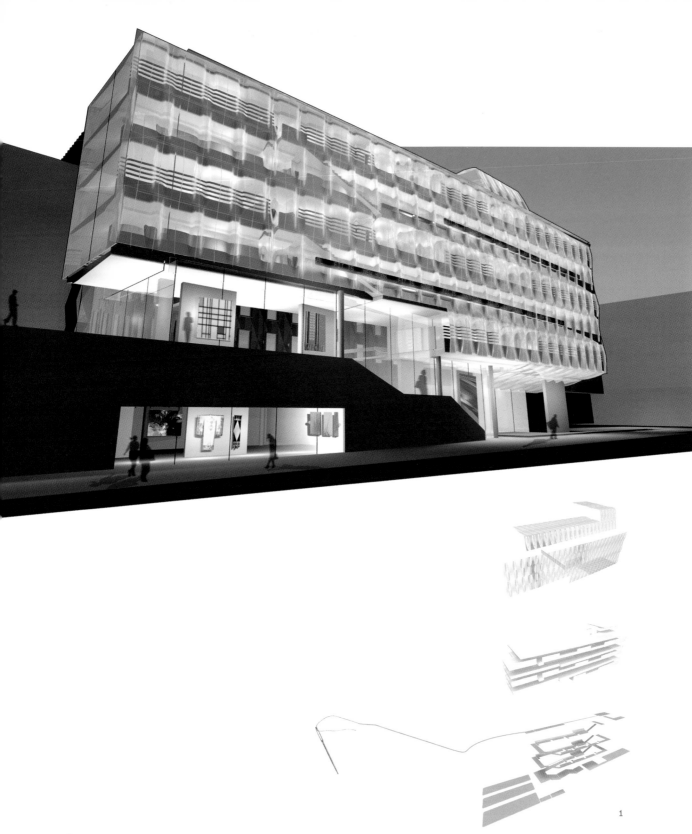

1

Well Dressed

The building has three principal components: a permeable, woven-glass membrane that forms a weather shield; an inner shell that encloses classrooms and offices; and a circulation thread, conducive to social congregation, that is lined with upholstered surfaces.

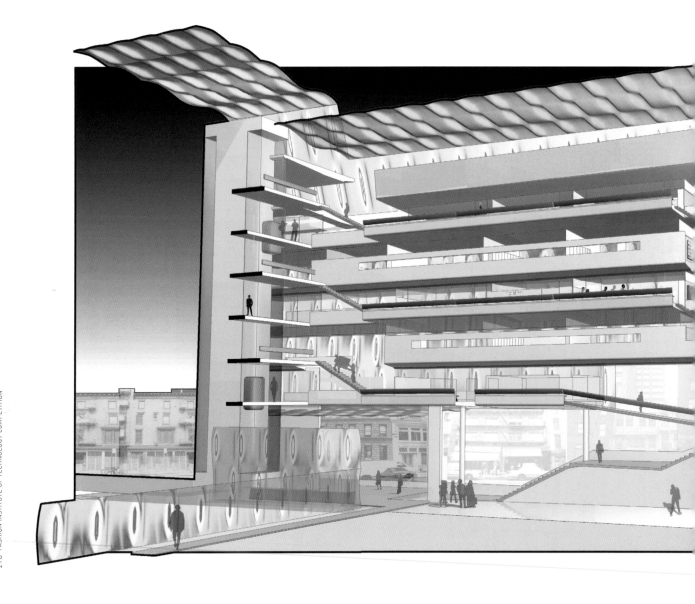

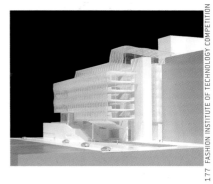

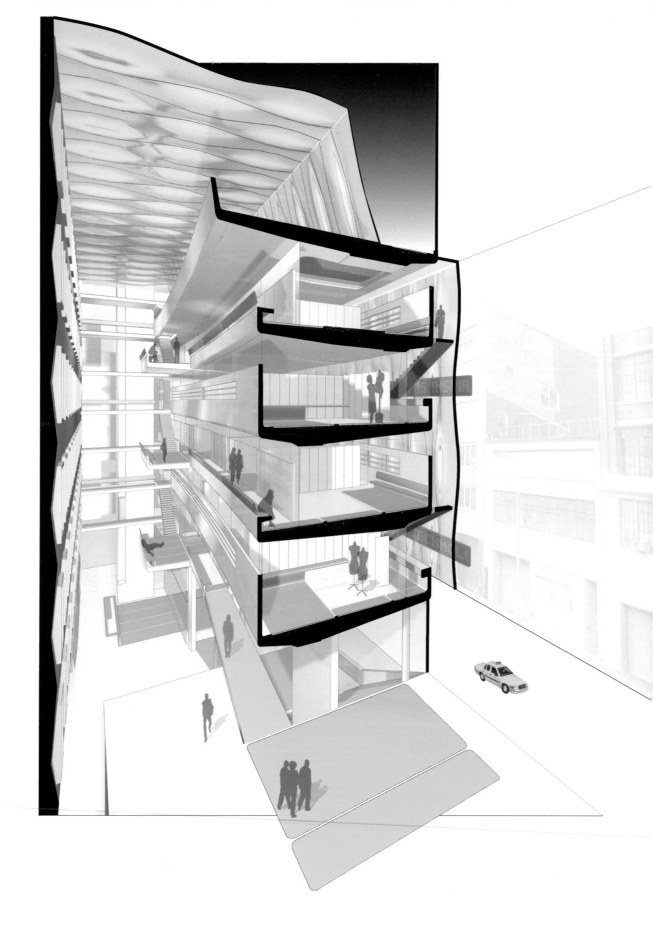

2

2
Glass Weave
The translucent woven-glass facade updates the bronze paneling of the C Building, which resembles a pleated textile. The new facade, like the old, is fabricated from a pattern, a modular element that repeats and reverses to create the effect of a continuous woven surface. A digital display employing commercial signage technologies threads its way through the glass weave, transmitting images and messages to viewers both inside and outside the building.

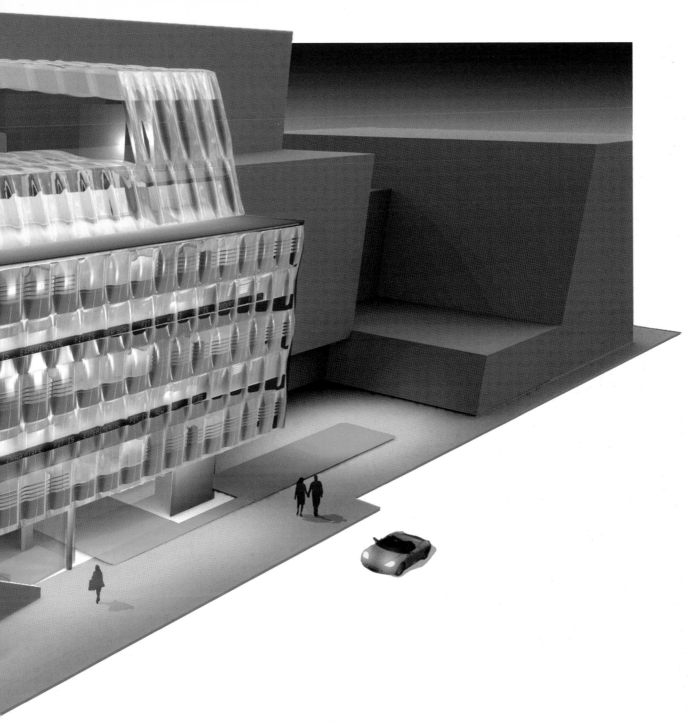

OLYMPIC EQUESTRIAN FACILITY STATEN ISLAND, NEW YORK, 2003– (WITH BALMORI ASSOCIATES)

As part of New York City's bid to host the 2012 Olympic Games, the organizing committee, NYC2012, invited us and the landscape firm Balmori Associates to design a sustainable equestrian facility for La Tourette Park on Staten Island. The design challenge was twofold: to create an economical (making use of off-the-shelf elements like bleachers and tents) but nevertheless memorable temporary equestrian facility and to leave behind an environmentally progressive park for future generations of New Yorkers.

Our proposal, rather than scattering isolated structures on the earth, weaves together buildings and landscape. The scheme is composed of two principal elements, a berm and a ribbon. The berm, an S-shaped earth mound, defines two outdoor spaces dedicated to spectatorship: a grass amphitheater that provides a podium for a demountable stadium for thirty-five thousand and a gently curving overlook that offers behind-the-scenes glimpses of warm-up fields where horses and riders are framed against a backdrop of marshlands. Stables for two hundred horses are embedded within the mound.

Threading its way through the berm, the ribbon performs two functions: it defines a public circulation route that links public stadium and private practice area and, at the same time, clads the principal programmatic elements, creating a translucent facade for the stadium, a covered canopy for VIP and press seating, and a pedestrian bridge that terminates in a roof terrace over the stables. Vertical incisions within this roof membrane permit natural light and views to pass between spectators above and athletes and animals below. A pattern of benday dots printed on the scrim that wraps the temporary bleachers merges with an identical pattern of planted dots scattered horizontally across the landscape, blurring the boundary between building and berm.

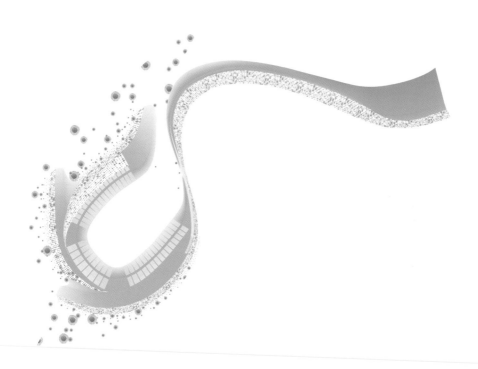

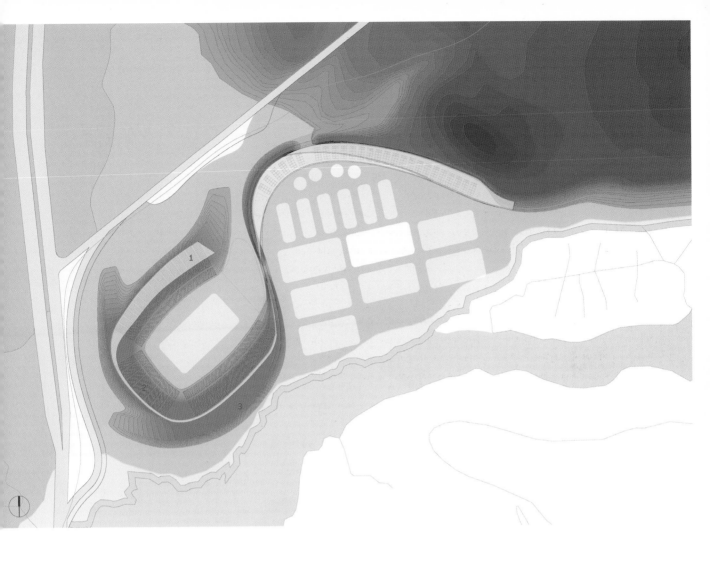

1

2

3

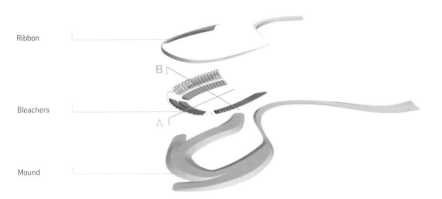

Ribbon

B

Bleachers

A

Mound

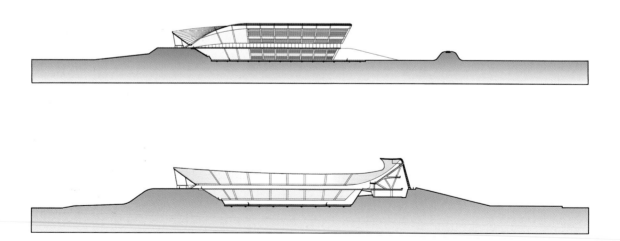

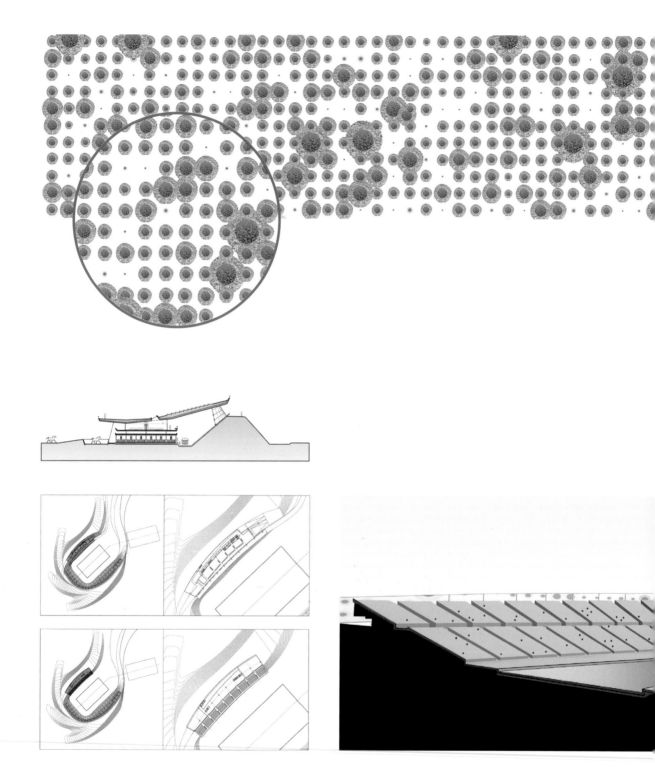

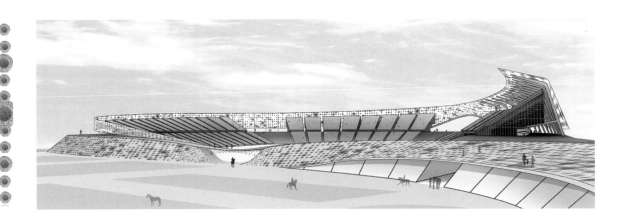

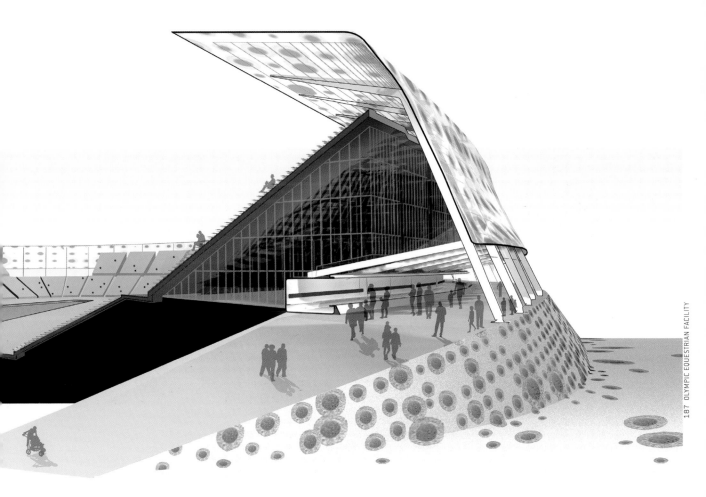

CREDITS

KYLE RESIDENCE
PROJECT ARCHITECT
Marc Tsurumaki
DESIGN TEAM
Dillon Kyle
Sean Keller

SIGHT SPECIFIC
PROJECT ARCHITECT
Marc Tsurumaki
DESIGN TEAM
Rachel Grey
Joanne Liou

PEEKSKILL ARTIST'S LIVE-WORK HOUSING
PROJECT ARCHITECT
Marc Tsurumaki
DESIGN TEAM
Joanne Liou
Christoph Roselius

ZIMENT ASSOCIATES
PROJECT ARCHITECT
Marc Tsurumaki
PROJECT TEAM
Kim Yao
Joanne Liou

HOUSE FOR A BACHELOR
PROJECT ARCHITECT
Claes Applequist
DESIGN TEAM
Charles Stone
Cedric Cornu

LEE LOFT
PROJECT ARCHITECT
Charles Stone
PROJECT TEAM
Alexandra Utsch
Marc Tsurumaki

VITALE LOFT
PROJECT ARCHITECT
Charles Stone
PROJECT TEAM
Christoph Roselius
Federico Algegria

FIVE MINUTE BATHROOM
PROJECT ARCHITECT
Christoph Roselius
PROJECT TEAM
Federico Algegria

SANDS LOFT
PROJECT ARCHITECT
Christoph Roselius

THE FOUNDRY
PROJECT ARCHITECT
Christoph Roselius
PROJECT TEAM
Charles Stone
Brian Kimura
Dan Gallagher
Adam Dayem

ACCESS HOUSE
PROJECT ARCHITECT
Dan Gallagher
PROJECT TEAM
Brian Kimura
Sung Kim
Brandon Hicks
Dan Marshall
Victor Kolesnichenko

MILLENNIUM RESIDENCE
PROJECT ARCHITECT
Brian Kimura
PROJECT TEAM
Adam Dayem
Christoph Roselius
Charles Stone

960 FOOD
PROJECT ARCHITECT
Brian Kimura
PROJECT TEAM
Dan Marshall

24/7 BUSINESS HOTEL
DESIGN TEAM
Brian Kimura
Paulo Faria

OLYMPIC TRAINERS
DESIGN TEAM
Brian Kimura
Edowa Shimizu
Damen Hamilton
Hiro Kashiwagi

EASYHOTEL

PROJECT ARCHITECT
Brian Kimura
PROJECT TEAM
Damen Hamilton
Edowa Shimizu

CHARLES WORTHINGTON NEW YORK

PROJECT ARCHITECT
Damen Hamilton
PROJECT TEAM
Brian Kimura
Edowa Shimizu

FASHION INSTITUTE OF TECHNOLOGY COMPETITION

ASSOCIATE ARCHITECT
RKTB: Carmi Bee, Principal
LANDSCAPE ARCHITECT
Balmori Associates: Diana Balmori,
Principal
ENERGY
Atelier 10
STRUCTURAL ENGINEER
Arup
CURTAIN WALL
C-Tek
PROJECT ARCHITECT
Brian Kimura
DESIGN TEAM
Edowa Shimizu
Damen Hamilton
Ariane Sphikas
Daniel Lopez
Cedric Cornu
Karen Tamir (Balmori Associates)
Anat Wilder (RKTB)
Calvin Lin (RKTB)
Jaejun Ryu (RKTB)

OLYMPIC EQUESTRIAN FACILITY

LANDSCAPE ARCHITECT
Balmori Associates: Diana Balmori,
Principal
STRUCTURAL ENGINEER
Arup
PROJECT ARCHITECT
Brian Kimura
DESIGN TEAM
Serra Kiziltan
Mark Thomann (Balmori Associates)
Sangmok Kim (Balmori Associates)

ILLUSTRATION CREDITS

Peter Aaron: cover, 35–39, 81, 84,
85, 103–7, 113–19, 135–43
Steven Barker: 20
Antoine Bootz: 82, 83
Edward Engelman: 50, 58, 59, 63
Leonard Fink: 51
Nikolas Koenig: 167–73
Dick Loesh/Courtesy Wexner
Center for the Arts, "House Rules"
exhibition, 1994: 23, 24
Bruce T. Martin: 46
Andrew Moore: 48
Jesus Moreno/Courtesy Galerie
Analix, Geneva: 45
Graziella Pazzanese: 154
Mark Robbins: 89, 91, 93, 95
Rick Scanlan: 73
Nic Tenwiggenhorn/Courtesy
Barbara Gladstone Gallery: 49
Courtesy Special Collections,
U.S. Air Force Academy, Colorado
Springs: 44
Kirk Winslow: 31